Finding What's Missing

Marco Lomax

First print 2018 June

ISBN-13: 978-1984157676
ISBN-10: 1984157671

Book Cover Design: Anointed Press Graphics, Inc

Book Productions: Crystell Publications
We Help You Self Publish Your Book
(405) 414-3991

Printed in the U.S.A.

DEDICATION

This book is dedicated to all the men & women that struggle with nonstop poor decision-making. It has also been written to bring awareness to all of the individuals who continue to receive chance after chance, yet keep going in and out of prison. This book is for those who fear change, and love to remain comfortable; for the parents that are setting good examples, but are not having sit-downs with their children to offer them quality time on discussions about life changing matters; and for the individuals who do not hold themselves accountable for their actions and are constantly running from life's challenges, opposed to facing them. This book is for you.

This book is also for the youth of today that are headed in the wrong direction. Recognize that it's never too late to change your mentality. For those who have been counted out. I encourage you to **NEVER GIVE IN & NEVER GIVE UP**. Believe in yourself first. Don't let anyone tell you that you can't make it.

This is for every man, woman, and juvenile that's locked up in the struggle. No matter where you are, you can still affect another person's life. Keep fighting and use your time wisely. Last but not least, this book is for anyone who is searching for what's missing within your life, and has yet to find it!!

CONTENTS

ACKNOWLEDGMENTS

First and foremost, I would like to thank God the father and my Lord and Savior Jesus Christ for leading me on a journey towards the completion of this book. My mother Lillian Patricia Sumler, for being the best mother a child could have. Thank you for always supporting me in every endeavor I've ever done. To Pop, you are the true definition of a Man of God. I appreciate all of your advice and everything that you have embedded within me.

To my lovely lady, Latoya, thank you for showing me what true love is. At the most detrimental time of my life, you re-entered and stayed with me for the whole ride. You are really a blessing from God and my true best friend. I love you more than you'll ever know.

Uncle Walt, you are truly my role model and a solid example of staying strong. Thank you for showing me what NEVER GIVING IN & NEVER GIVING UP looks like.

To my brother Rodney, I'm proud of you bruh; you came a long way and your work is still not done; (Be Safe, No Doubt, Luv!) My brother Shawn, we've been through a lot together and still standing tall. Trea, I love you Lil sis; stay focused and away from the fakes and the phonies. Tev, thanks for always encouraging me. Lil Carol, you are an accurate classification of a strong black woman. You and Morgan are always in my prayers. Big Cuz, you helped me out a lot in my lifetime, and I will never forget that. Lil Roland, you never let me down, much love lil cuz.

It's impossible for me to name everyone, but to all of my family, friends, and everyone that affected my life in a positive or negative way, please know that you only made me stronger and wiser.

R.I.P. Aunt Carol, you'll forever be missed. My dad, Vernon Lee Lomax, R.I.P, thank you for my laid-back, stand up temperament. Dr. Walls, you've inspired me in so many ways, keep fighting bruh, God has a lot of work for you. Goo, thanks for encouraging me to complete this assignment. L.A., thanks for reading and giving me insight on my work.

Lastly, to all who made this book possible, thank you for your assistance!

FOREWARD

In order to find what's missing in one's life, an individual must be willing to go through a stringent process of searching to discover and learn what is needed. Something or someone has disappeared, or has been lost; therefore, a search party is called to find what's missing.

This autobiography will take you on a journey of a young man whose story will inspire the reader to stay connected to vital information handed down from those who care about and love you. It's important these days to take heed from those who have foresight, basically – "been there and done that", if you know what I mean. Contrary to the new societal norm; if you don't have a vision, you'll perish.

I challenge the reader to think of your current situation. Is this good for me or not? Make the right choices, plan for your today and tomorrow. Stand up and fight against your giant(s).

After all, in the end, what's missing is finding you.

~Dr. Jachin B. Walls, Sr.

"Those who profess to favor freedom and yet depreciate agitation, are people who want crops without plowing the ground; they want rain without the roar of its many waters. The struggle may be a moral one, or it may be a physical one, or it may be both. But it must be a struggle. Power concedes nothing without a demand; it never has, and it never will."

~Frederick Douglass

1

HOW IT STARTS

"You Create Your Own Experience."

As children growing up, being loved and accepted is what we mainly look for from others. Although that may be difficult to receive, we'll do whatever we think it takes to obtain that love and acceptance. While most households don't have both parents within them, feelings of abandonment or not being loved is subconsciously birthed early on within the average family. It's a natural feeling to know when something is missing; however figuring it out is not that easy. Despite the fact that my biological dad was killed when I was still an infant, fortunately, I grew up with two parents within my household. And even still with that, I always felt it was something always missing. Nevertheless, putting a finger on it seemed impossible. Being young and not knowing at the time that the man raising me was not my biological father, still allowed me to have an emotional void. While some kids have those men in their lives who lead them down the road of demolition by either various forms of domestic violence, the act of dealing and using drugs, profane language towards them, and other behaviors that lack character, my father figure actually exemplified for me what a real man does. He always worked, ensured that his wife and blended family were taken care of, and was a quality man of God who was respectful to us as well as to others. Now with a better understanding of the man that served as my father figure, I'm sure some of you are reading this and wondering what was I possibly missing?

In regards to being a little boy, there are a lot of things he needs to learn from a man in order to fully understand what should and should not take place throughout his life. Young boys need to learn how to groom themselves, the importance of giving a firm handshake, and how to treat a woman. Learning these characteristics early on are very significant towards their growth as an adult. Without these things being taught, young boys will most likely pick up what they see. Sometimes they adopt these behaviors without knowing if it's the right way to go or not.

While the man in my life displayed through his actions how to treat a woman, there was still a lot missing that I wasn't aware of. The fact that I had older brothers also put me in a position to pick up a lot of what I saw them doing. While I was the youngest of six boys, it was only natural for me to imitate what was being seen. So learning how to ride a bike and getting introduced to sports, all came from observing what was close to me.

Let me clarify something as well, imitating and being taught are two totally different ways of learning something. You can also be taught something and still be misled. When adults fail to sit down and explain the do's and don'ts of life to young boys and girls, they are put in a greater position to encounter some very detrimental circumstances. Take for instance a young boy who's never been properly introduced to sex; with so much on the internet, he'll more than likely learn from there. If not there, he'll imitate what is seen and heard from his peers. With that, it could potentially lead to him establishing a disrespectful viewpoint of women, which in the long run could result in him never understanding the value and impact of the woman. As he gets older, even if he may have some awareness on how to treat a woman, he won't necessarily see the wrong in his disrespectful ways. This example alone is the reason why I believe "sit downs" with kids are very essential. Being afraid to give them knowledge will only hurt them in the long run. Of course, there is a time for everything, but avoiding that time should never be the case.

I've mentioned before that the man in my life did display through his actions how to treat a woman, but that "sit down" was never there. It didn't take place until I became a conscious young man who fully understood that what he displayed was an accurate qualification of a man. Having a close relationship with the father figure or the mother figure in a child's life is extremely necessary. Without that continuous support, that missing feeling will spread with no explanation.

I remember the first time I played football for the Peppermill Pirates at the age of 11. Our team was undefeated until we went to the playoffs. While most of my teammates had their dads on the sidelines during some of our practices and mostly all of our games, I would ride with a friend and his dad and hang out with them afterwards. Now at the time, I was aware that my biological dad was deceased. My father figure may have attended some of my games, however I wasn't receiving from him the attention a child may need growing up. Mainly this was because I wasn't the only child and for him, the household necessities came first. Even still, I wasn't aware of the emotional void I had within. Eventually, it led me to seeking acceptance from my peers and wanting to hang out more outside of my home.

Learning about my dad's past has been a major influence on my life, and it pretty much shaped my way of thinking. Reflecting back on the first time I originally heard of the man whose blood flows through my body, it placed me in the mind frame of being just like him. While I didn't take on every aspect of his life, I did take on the street mentality I heard he possessed, and I did it proudly. Actually, I did it not even considering what I fully was getting into.

I was originally born in Baltimore, but moved to Seat Pleasant, Maryland at a very young age. I'm sure my mother's intention was to remove us from the same environment that my dad was a product of only to gradually find out that I became accustomed to the same lifestyle within an environment that was supposed to keep me from being a statistic. Of course, it was only a matter of time before I'd learn of my father, but my mom didn't want his past to shape my life, so she did everything she could possibly do to shield me from what she knew wasn't any good for me. Her experiences growing up that revolved around a time period I couldn't even imagine, plus her experiences with my dad's street lifestyle and untimely death, she knew what my final outcome could be. Like it's always been said, when you choose the streets, you're either going to end up dead or locked up, and death was something my mom had to face with a man she loved and the father of her three sons. Me being so young and naive, I was unaware of the pain I would subconsciously cause myself and my loved ones as I was being influenced and fascinated by all the wrong things.

5

Growing up in the county was not the same as my city experience. The county is not as fast paced as the city, and the neighborhoods are not as bad. Being a part of both of these environments, I saw how some kids are less fortunate than others, including myself. That feeling alone can cause a lack of self-confidence and you just want to fit in with the crowd and not be left out. While in my household, we strived to maintained what we truly needed, as far as food, clothes and electricity, I just wanted more than we could actually afford. Like some of the youth I grew up with, I couldn't say that I didn't have food to eat. Actually, getting Popeyes on some Sundays after church seemed liked the best meal ever. I never needed clothes either, and though they may have been hand-me-downs from older relatives, or items my parents purchased from the thrift store, I always had something to wear. Most often, my shoes came from Payless, so seeing other kids wearing designer clothes and shoes only made me want them as well. In time, what I've learned is that those things were items I wanted, not really what I needed. However, seeing my older brother whom I shared my room with, get slick things influenced me even more. The more I was around the more fortunate, and older guys, the more it made me want to do something about it.

When I became a teenager, that's when I started to have serious behavioral problems, as well as my initial contact with law enforcement. Since I wanted the latest sneakers and clothing brands that were hot at the time, I knew I'd have to figure out how to get them. Plus, to add additional stress, at this point in my life, females were becoming a priority and more appealing than ever. That led to me wanting to impress an even larger population of people all for the sake of fitting in. Aware of the fact that my parents were just making ends meet, it was obvious that the expensive clothes and footwear would not be put before the household necessities. So, I figured out how I could get them myself. The first thing I needed to do was get a job, so I started working at a barbershop sweeping hair in *Mitchellville Plaza.*

It felt good to make my own money, but I must admit that my taste was so expensive that I would have to save for a couple of weeks in order to buy a whole outfit. At this time, since I was still growing, I'd also wear some of my brother's clothes and shoes, while I got my plan together. Yet, once again, observing others who were making money so easily, it increased my desire to do the exact same thing. After working for a while, I accumulated a few dollars, but I felt like I wasn't moving forward. As a result of my youthfulness, I was not really aware of the fact that I was going to put myself in a position that would result in a long-term setback.

Trying to make life changes, I decided to purchase and sell marijuana to quickly flip my money. I saved my money to avoid owing anyone for whatever drugs I received. Now of course I didn't know exactly what I would make off of it, so I had to learn the ins and outs of the drug game. However, after learning how to weigh and bag weed, I would sell out fast and end up making triple what I made in the barbershop. Here's an example of being inadequately taught and misled!

As most know, exposure brings about curiosity, so since I was out dealing, I eventually started smoking marijuana. And because everyone around me was doing it, it was difficult to resist. With money coming in so quickly and easily, and the amount of clothes and fresh sneakers I was buying, I started telling my mom lies as to where I was getting all my new stuff from. Well, my mother was no fool, so she knew I was smoking weed and selling drugs. She was a woman of God and had lived long enough to know when her children were making bad decisions. I'm sure she saw some of my dad's behavior were within me.

Determined to be in the streets, I eventually got busted with drugs in school, which resulted in my mom coming to get me. In spite of being caught, of course I continued to lie, saying the drugs weren't mine, and that I was holding them for someone else. Thinking back on it right now, I can see how foolish I probably looked, but at the time it sounded believable.

My actions caused me to get put out of school, and I ended up going to an alternative school. The decisions that I was making didn't just affect me, but my parents as well. Going to this alternative school caused my parents to re-adjust their schedules for me to ensure that getting my education was a priority. They had to drop me off and pick me up from school, especially, since part of the punishment caused me to be on home monitoring by the courts.

Now this was my first encounter with law enforcement and my

first trip to jail. Notice how I said first, because it surely wasn't my last. That was just how it started.

2

THE SEARCH

"What we see depends mainly on what we look for."
-John Lubbock

After being placed on home monitoring, it was a must for me to stay out of trouble to avoid going to *Boys' Village of Maryland*, which is a prison for juveniles. While I was able to go back to my original school, I still wasn't taking my education serious enough. At that moment in my life, I was searching for who I wanted to be. Trying to fit in and letting the wrong things influence me was what got me into trouble in the first place, so you would think that I would have learned from my mistakes. However, I had so much more to learn. I wasn't even aware of how much my poor decision making was hurting me, and I wasn't even paying attention to the cause and effects.

Growing up, I was a pretty good basketball player. I was tall and most certainly not the average teenager's height. One day while I was playing basketball during an open gym session, the high school basketball coach was watching and approached me afterwards with an offer to play on his team. Sadly, my troubles wouldn't allow me to play because I had to be home after school. However, once I was removed from home detention, the position was still available for me. I played about eight games, but by me not taking my education seriously, I was removed from the team. My grade point average didn't reach the required standard to play on the team, and as a result of that I could've gotten all the games I played in with the team forfeited. That comes from focusing on the wrong things and is an example of how your actions affect others as well. I let my team down and myself. As a result of no longer being busy, I went back to

9

what got me arrested, the streets. See, playing basketball was fun, but it wasn't giving me what I was searching for. Honestly, I didn't even know what I was searching for, but I can say that wanting the things that weren't important led to one poor decision after another.

Although I had love and acceptance within my home, something was still missing, and I continued searching to fill that void. While in high school I met this beautiful girl, who in time I pretty much fell in love with. It was something special about her, but I couldn't put my finger on it. Yet, though I knew she was into me, I didn't exactly know how much. Likewise, even though I saw how my father figure treated my mom, I imitated how my peers and the older guys in the streets treated their females. I saw them being in relationships with more than one girl at a time and I did the same thing. You see not having that "sit down" with my father figure, along with the poor illustration I witnessed from others, hindered me from some essential information on how I should treat a female. My lack of understanding of how to treat a female and not knowing how she truly felt about me caused me to hurt this young girl's feelings. I wasn't intentionally doing it, I just thought what I was doing was the norm and the committed relationship that my mom and father figure had was an older folk's fad. At the time, I didn't know that I had actually found my true love. So being naïve to that, I ended up losing a good girl. We were together on and off throughout high school, but while I was running the streets searching for more money and happiness, she eventually moved on in life.

As I continued to run the streets, I started to make a nice amount of cash and was able to support myself. I thought I had all the answers. The more money I made, the bigger my head got; and no matter how many times I was arrested, I went back to doing the same thing. Not consciously aware of this, I was searching for a real prison sentence. Luckily, someone was praying for me, because in my earlier arrests, I either got my cases dismissed or received probation. After learning of my dad's lifestyle, and then having other family members as well as peers go in and out of jail, that's what I thought being a man was all about. Since I was making money and doing a lot on my own, I thought I was living out what some coin as "true manhood." Well, that may have been what I was after, but life and time has taught me different.

Now I don't want to be misunderstood, because jail wasn't a part of the plan. I just knew that came with the lifestyle I'd chosen for myself, and if I got caught, I would just have to deal with the consequences. Of course I never thought I'd get caught, even after the first time I was arrested, I figured I'd outsmart the law the next time.

Having a criminal mentality is unfavorable to one's life, you're constantly searching for better ways to be a criminal. Is that insane or what? It is, and I hope I'm making it clear that when you're seeking love and acceptance in the wrong places, the wrong perspective on life is what you end up getting.

I was raised in a household of God-fearing parents, and going to church was a must under their roof, and abiding by their rules came along with it. Although I stayed in church growing up and had loving parents that provided me with what I needed, I still managed to search for everything outside of my home. The funny thing about it, Proverbs 22:6 states: "Train up a child in the way he should go, and when he is old he will not depart from it." As you continue to read, you'll understand how that scripture speaks to my life.

For most of my adolescence I searched for ways to make more money. Not knowing my love for money was going to be a downfall for me, I figured it would bring me happiness. It seems like the more money I made, the more I spent or loss due to my illegitimate way of living. While I'm searching for riches in the wrong way, I continued to lose more and more. Instead, I should have educated myself and learned how to invest in legal endeavors in order to experience a way of living that would bring me true wealth. I can't fault myself as I didn't know any better, so learning the hard way was meant for me. Any other way wouldn't have taught me the lessons I've learned today. As I continued to fall short, I kept on searching for guidance because of my ambition for a better life, at least what I thought was better.

Searching for popularity and having a name for yourself is what most young people want. So putting me in the position to be remembered is what I woke up for. Not knowing that I'd be talked about no matter what I did. I didn't want to be joked on in a bad way by any means, I just wanted to be considered cool. Of course if I'm out there selling drugs, not only do I have to have nice clothes and shoes, but a vehicle was a must although I did not have a driver's license. I don't think I even need to express how not having a license wasn't going to stop me, because I've already made it clear that I wasn't obeying the law anyway. Plus, my mindset was the same as not getting caught selling drugs. I just knew I wouldn't get pulled over, and I didn't. However, I had to continue to lie to my mother, because how could I let her know that I had a car without a driver's license and a legal job?

The first vehicle I purchased was a two-door Oldsmobile, Delta 88. It was clean as a whistle! While my drug dealing skills seemed to bring me success, I was gradually moving up to the level of the guys I was looking up to. I would go out to different events such as go-go parties, cabarets and cookouts in my own wheels which made me feel like the man. Sadly, I was getting myself deeper and deeper into the street life. Thoughts of being a scientist, mechanic, engineer, or even playing professional basketball was never on my mind. Actually, fast money had blind folds over my eyes. Daily, it forced me to continually search for the right now. I had false hopes of getting rich that way, instead of searching for sustained success.

This way of thinking continued for years, and allowing myself to get attached to mammon caused me to not fully understand the value of life. I knew right from wrong; however, as crazy as this may sound, some things that were wrong seemed right, and that was my reality. I did continue to stay in school, school actually was fun. And by me trying to impress others, I wanted to show them that I was considered a big boy. At least I thought I was by attending the high school football and basketball games in fly gear and driving my own car. See most kids in my high school rode the bus and if they were driving, their parents either gave them a car or brought it for them. So I felt like the fact that I brought my car with my own money, well, that made me a man. But in all reality, it didn't make me anything but a confused young boy. Seeking the status of manhood, when I should have been enjoying the life of a teenager had me headed in the wrong direction. The more I hung around those confused like-minded individuals, as well as the older guys on the block who set bad examples for all the youngsters in the hood, the more I got sucked into the street life.

I never really took my education seriously, but I did manage to still graduate from high school. Now I wasn't ignorant by far, I just wasn't applying myself in the way I should have. Even though I did do my work sometimes, I would either pay for it to be done, or by me being popular, some girl would do it for me or give me the answers. This was a bad skill that I obtained, because as I got older, I continued to use the same philosophy to get through life.

As I reflect now, I realize that that's not how life operates. Hard work and dedication are how one succeeds. See, nothing in life is given to you. No matter what; you have to put in work. I may have been receiving fast money, but I still was putting in work to get it. I was just putting the right kind of energy into a negative way of living. If I had put that same energy into playing basketball, I may be an NBA player today, opposed to an inmate. Basketball is most certainly a gift that I have. I mean, I'm naturally a good player, and had I trained and focused on bettering myself, who knows where I would be right now. By me focusing on the right now and not thinking about the future, my future turned out to be one that exists behind prison walls. And guess what? I'm still searching for what I was missing.

The search will never end as long as you're alive and breathing. You should always be searching for greatness, and if you're in a place in your life where you're fully satisfied, then set your eyes on someone to help you move to the next level. Self-improvement should always be on your agenda. See there are a lot of youth running around searching for who they would like to be. Without the proper teaching, sit-downs, and great examples, they will continue searching for the wrong things and may possibly end up here where I am, or buried in a grave.

I'm blessed to be able to still be searching, because I know a lot of individuals who would love to be in my shoes, maybe not behind these prison walls, but by having a second chance to make a turnaround. That second chance should not be taken lightly. That's why I'm writing this book today. I've taken my life for granted for many years, but I realized once you know better, you must do better. So as I continue to search for greatness, helping others may be my tool for my success.

3

FROM BAD TO WORSE

"You cannot change what you do not acknowledge."
-Unknown

After graduating high school, I didn't have too much of a plan. I was already making money, so getting a job or going to college wasn't even a thought. While still living under my parents' roof, I had to consider getting a job, because not doing anything with myself wasn't going to be acceptable. Personally, I didn't feel any real pressure to get a job, so I pretended as if I was actually looking for one. However, I was still in the streets, and I knew my parents knew what I was doing, because I wasn't asking them for anything. So how else was I surviving? They were just making it and they both had jobs, so for me to be coming and going as if everything was alright, it showed that I was still doing the same ole thing of selling drugs.

For a while I didn't have to contribute to anything in the house, so the money I was making was all mine. Even though I was out buying food and things, I still was able to eat when I was at home. Since my mother knew where I was getting my money, I couldn't offer any of it for things around the house. Her Christian principles wouldn't allow her to accept it.

I started slipping up more and more every day because smoking marijuana and drinking alcohol was clouding my judgment. There was a time when I had a safe in my room, and I would put some of my drugs in there. Thinking it would never be found, I would stash the key to the safe in the bathroom under the carpet, and it seemed like the perfect spot. Shortly after entering the house one day, my mother had my safe open with the key and my drugs exposed. I was shocked that she was able to find the key. Of course I lied once again and told her I was holding the drugs for a friend while he was out of town. She wasn't buying it and told me to get the stuff out of her house. She also told me not to ever bring them back. I didn't pay her fussing or frustration any mind. I was just glad she didn't destroy the drugs. After this incident, getting a job was a must if I was going to remain in that house.

As I started seeking some type of employment, my plan was to work and still sell drugs. I would have my mom off of my back, and I still would be bringing in the amount of cash a job couldn't provide. Since I was involved with a lot of people through my dealings, an associate put me down with a company hiring for the trash removal and recycling. I went and applied for the job, was hired, and started out as a temporary Trash Truck Helper. I eventually became permanent on the recycling truck as a helper. With me recently receiving my driver's license, it helped me with my permanent position, because the trash truck drivers needed to hold a commercial driver's license (CDL), and this was not a requirement working on the recycling truck. Although I wasn't hired as a driver, if an emergency had taken place, I was capable of driving. Plus, my assigned driver was cool and allowed me to drive at times. He was from D.C. and had a street life mentality, so of course we clicked because I was still in the streets myself. A lot of our routes we had were in the D.C. area, and the neighborhood he was from was one of them. Whenever we finished our route for the day, which some days were shorter than others, we still got paid for eight hours, which I liked. If our route wasn't too heavy, this allowed us a lot of free time. With the spare time we had, the both of us were still able to sell our drugs and shoot dice around his neighborhood with his buddies. This job thing seemed better than I expected. My current situation seemed to be on the rise, but in reality, it was getting ready to crash.

Still having my foot in the streets, ducking and dodging the police were always a part of the job. When you have times where you get away with selling drugs for a while, it's inevitable that it wouldn't last forever. Knowing that I had a warrant for my arrest, quitting my job went without saying. All it would have taken was for me to either be going to or getting off work to be arrested. So I ended up quitting my job, but I continued to allow my mother to believe that I was still working. In order for me to get my last check, I had to turn in my uniforms, so this had to be done without my mother knowing.

One day I had a friend of mine come through the back alley of my house; I dropped my uniforms down to him and met him in the parking lot. Once I returned them, I still continued to act as if I was going to work. By me being wanted, I wouldn't stay at home at night; I would just stop in periodically during the day. While staying at different friend's houses, I wouldn't stop by my mother's house until the time I usually got off of work.

The way I found out that I had a warrant in the first place was from some friends and I being stopped by the police one night. We all gave them our I.D.'s, but the officers slipped up by giving me back my I.D. and letting me go. They had mistaken one of my friends for me. Due to us having a total different description, specifically in height, I don't know how they did that. As I heard my name coming through the police radio and me having a warrant for my arrest, I begin to walk away until I was out of their eyesight, and then I ran faster than ever. Knowing that they would realize they had let me go, I figured they would go by my house. As I watched from the back path to my house, two officers knocked on the door, and ended up speaking with my mother. Once they learned I was not there, they left. I immediately went home once I saw them leave. I wanted to find out what was said.

The officers didn't let my mother know that I had a warrant, they didn't even mention that I was just stopped by them. They just told her they wanted to speak with me when I was available. I gave my mother no indication that I was in any type of trouble. The heads up was truly helpful on my end, because I knew I had to move light so I wouldn't go back to jail. By me remaining low key, the police continued calling and stopping by my house. To stop the stress this was causing my mother, I ended up turning myself in.

Once in the custody of the police, they questioned me for a few, and as I continued to have nothing to say, they eventually just sent me to the detention center. By me no longer being a juvenile, my mother couldn't just come and get me to bring me home. I had to go through the adult process by seeing the commissioner and seeing if I'd receive bail or not. Unfortunately, I didn't receive bail after speaking with the commissioner. My prior history with law enforcement played a major part in that decision. The next move was to get a lawyer, so when I went to court, I could request bail. With me not being measured a flight risk, when I went to court, bail was pre-arranged. After sitting in jail for approximately 120 days throughout this whole process, my bail was paid, and I was a free man again.

Having the experience of going to jail as a juvenile, you would think I wouldn't want to continue to make the same bad decisions. Now that I was an adult, the penalty was much more severe, so trying something different should have been on my to do list. Instead, I continued to travel down the wrong road, going from bad to worse. My behavior as well as my way of thinking wasn't getting any better. The more trouble I got into, the more I thought about doing it better than the last time. That criminal mentality was taking a hold on my mind. I mean, what was I thinking about? I'd been in the same situation several times and I continued to keep getting the same results. Even though I kept getting the same results and still wasn't changing, something was truly missing, and I still didn't have a clue. I was smart enough to know I needed to do better, but by my thoughts being influenced by negativity, it showed I had nothing on my mind. I didn't have any goals or plans for the future; I thought selling drugs was going to bring me success. Having that mindset as a juvenile was bad, but thinking like that as an adult was even worse. These poor decisions I was making all played a significant part towards my future. It allowed me to see that if you continue to think the same, your circumstances will never change, so don't expect anything different.

If you're in a bad place in life, trying something different can help. It doesn't mean that you won't have trials and tribulations; however, going through tests only makes you stronger. Poor decisions are a part of the test in life. In order to pass and move on to the next exam, you have to study what's been holding you back in order to move forward. Having the outlook to make that change before your situation turns from bad to worse should be taken advantage of; if not, the worst may turn out to be more than you can envision. Maybe even more than you can handle. Remember, once you know better, you must do better, so don't ignore the signs. I ignored all the warning signals for many, many years. Fortunately, I still have the opportunity to right my wrongs. If you're reading this book and you know that you need to make some better decisions, don't hesitate, change now, before it is too late.

4

SAME MENTALITY, DIFFERENT LOCATION

"Where you are going ought to be
bigger than where you have been."
-Unknown

Upon my release from the detention center, change did cross my mind; however, it was only the change of my location, not my mentality. I had already thought about the decision while I was incarcerated, so a few hours after coming home, I went back to Baltimore. It was an easy move, due to the majority of my family living there. Having somewhere to stay wasn't going to be a problem. I knew I could just crash at a family member's house until I got on my feet to get my own place. Though I would only be staying there temporarily, it mainly would be just to shower and rest, because I was still chasing after money. My sister-in-law's house was the perfect location for me.

See, back when I was in school and I was expelled for being arrested with having drugs on my possession, my parents punished me and wouldn't allow me to talk on the phone, go outside or anything. Me being very rebellious, I ran away, caught the train to Baltimore and stayed at my sister-in-law's house along with my three nieces. It was much more freedom for me, especially since I thought I was grown. When I had to go to court, I ended up going back to my parent's house and that's when I was placed on home monitoring. Therefore, my sister-in-law and I already had a good rapport, and I knew staying with her wouldn't be a problem. She always took me in as if I was her biological brother, and the rest of her family did the same. Without even calling her, I arrived at her house to let her know I needed to stay there for a little while. She accepted me with open arms.

Once I moved back to Baltimore, I wasn't thinking about doing anything different than before. I figured that by being a new face around I wouldn't be targeted by the police. By me arriving with no belongings, I just felt I had to hustle much harder. Given that I had family in the streets as well, I just linked up with some of them to have a location to sell drugs. The same rules applied, this was just a different environment and I can admit money was flowing at a high velocity. The way things were operating, I wish I would've been moved back to Baltimore. I adapted quickly to life in Baltimore as if I grew up on those city corners my entire childhood. The money I was making in the county was much slower than this. In addition to there being much more excitement going on, city life seemed to be where it was at. Furthermore, me being a fresh face in the area, the females wanted to know who I was and where I had come from. They knew that I wasn't from the area, because they had been around those neighborhoods their entire lives. On top of that, my style of dress and accent wasn't considered the norm, they thought I talked country. Given that I was always a laid-back guy, I wasn't too caught up by the attention. My main focus was getting some money. Even though I had my encounters with the ladies, they still weren't a priority.

Pressed for cash and wanting to get into a more comfortable spot was my mission. While staying at my sister-in-law's place was cool, sleeping on the couch wasn't the way I wanted to live. Not that I hadn't done it before, but I wanted my own privacy, specifically my own bed. The money I was bringing in allowed me to save some cash to get an apartment. Having connections helped with that process tremendously, because without a job, that's pretty impossible to do. Most of the time when you're doing illegal things, your whole method of living is illegal, so being connected allowed me to be able to get an apartment in someone else's name. As long as the rent was paid on time, there would never be any problems. At this instant, no more sleeping on the couch, and I finally had a comfortable place to bring a female.

Getting another vehicle was my next move, due to me selling my car after being arrested back in the county. The cash was needed at the time and I didn't want to keep the car because people were easily identified by their vehicles. I'd already been in enough trouble, so if I would've stayed in the county, I wanted to be under the radar as much as possible. The good thing about the city, transportation was provided for you much easier than in the county. Despite the fact that the bus ran more frequently, that wasn't my travel of choice. Calling a sedan company or catching a hack (similar to a cab) wasn't expensive and you were taken to your direct location. This was the form of transportation used until I purchased a vehicle. I was able to save money because I would only get a ride to the block to sell drugs and back home once I was done for the day. All the going out and partying was put on hold until I had room for that. My mission wasn't going to be distracted by a bunch of wild partying. If I only would have used the mentality of not being distracted towards a positive mission! The most partying I did was smoke weed and drink alcohol. I considered that my reward for all the work I was putting in on those street corners. I reached my goal and was able to purchase a two-door, stick shift Nissan Sentra. Prior to purchasing it, I didn't know how to drive a stick shift so I had to teach myself how to drive it.

Even though I was staying in Baltimore, my case in the county was still pending. I made sure I appeared at my court date to avoid receiving an FTA (failure to appear). Due to me being out on bail, my bond could have easily been revoked for not appearing at my appointed time. For this reason, I attended my hearing to receive a postponement. Now, I'm trying to pick up where I left off, and things were going smoothly for me. I had my place, a car, and a money flow like never before. Since I wasn't living in the area I was dealing in, I felt much safer when I went home.

One thing I learned from being in the streets is that jealousy and envy comes with the territory. It is evident that when you're out in the streets, people are always watching. You must be alert at all times, but most of us are out there still smoking marijuana and drinking alcohol, unfocused, and we believe that we're on point. For those that are sober and law abiding citizens, their just outside looking in at us destroying ourselves. You couldn't have told me that back then, I just knew I was as sharp as a double-edged sword.

Growing up in Seat Pleasant, I traveled to Baltimore regularly to visit my grandparents, aunts, uncles and cousins. I just never indulged in any criminal activity during those visits. Me being an adult and back in the city for good, I was able to be in all the wrong places at the right time. See, the Baltimore neighborhood that I was living in prior to my family moving to Seat Pleasant was knocked down, so that's not where I was hanging out. I was hanging out on the blocks where my family members lived on or had lived in the past. Without a doubt I was a new face, and coming around taking money out of the pockets of guys who had been around for years wasn't liked at all. I wasn't a chump by far, I just wasn't known. This led to me being introduced to some friends that grew up with my family that had a name out in the streets. Having those guys around at times put a hold on the ones who wanted to try me. I was sharp enough to know that, so I would make sure that I kept my eyes open at all times.

While hanging out in the streets, I almost was never alone. One of my childhood friends came to Baltimore with me. By us having the same mentality, we stuck together through it all. I knew he would have my back if something went wrong and vice versa. We were together so much, some even thought we were brothers. He was even welcomed into most of my family member's homes as well. Constantly being together, we were able to pick up on things that one of us might have missed. With all the traffic and everything moving so fast, being on point was critical. After being around this neighborhood a short period of time, we started to take over the customers. We were providing the addicts with something different than what they were normally receiving.

I remember an incident when some guy pulled up across the street from my friend and I. I could hear him asking his buddies about us. He spoke on the fact that we weren't from the area, and as they huddled up, I told my friend we were going to have a problem. Just so happened while this took place, my brother came by to check on us, so I let him know what was going on. He left and came back with some of the same friends that were well known. As they got out of the car and greeted me and my homeboy, I saw the group of guys melt away. Those guys had a reputation for not being played with, so the next day, one of the guys from the neighborhood pulled me up and let me know there wasn't any problem with my friend and I. He explained that he didn't know who we were, and by us being friends with those guys, we were cool. Not being naive to the streets, I knew that that was a sign of fear, and you never know what a person of fear would do. Knowing that, my friend and I discussed getting a gun to protect ourselves from being robbed or killed, because I didn't trust that guy. After networking with a few people, we received a pistol and made sure we had it every day we went outside.

Feeling well protected had us staying around the neighborhood more hours than we normally had. We begin to hustle day and night, because that meant more cash. If we wouldn't stay on the block, we would end up going out. My female cousin was always partying with her friends, so my friend and I would go hang out with them most of the time. They knew where all the good clubs were. Having all these different connections assisted me with adapting to my new location. This pattern continued for some time, especially since my court date, stemming from my charge in Prince George's County, was coming up again. I wanted to have as much fun as possible, because I didn't truly know my fate when it came to my case. I always believed I would get off, but there was always a chance of me serving prison time.

In this instance, I was acquitted on all charges when I went back to court. I was enormously happy, officially a free man without any court dates or probation over my head. Ever since I was a juvenile, I remained in the judicial system. So being free as an adult was cause for a celebration. I partied for a few days and still kept the same mentality as if I would continue to outsmart the system. Relocating seemed like a great idea; however, not long after I got acquitted on one case, I was arrested for possession of a handgun in my new location. By this being my first arrest in this jurisdiction, a bail was set and immediately paid. Now I'm back in the same predicament I just got out of, facing a prison sentence.

When your mentality stays the same, it doesn't matter where you relocate to. Everything starts with your mind and as you think, so you will be. As I continued to believe that moving from one environment to another and committing the same acts were going to give me different outcomes, it only had me bamboozled and in need of being redeveloped for my purpose. My decision-making was only setting me up for hard times in the future. The more I continued to get into trouble, the harder it was for me to get out. You don't see those things in that moment, that's why listening to those who have been there and done that is very important. Their wisdom and experience is much greater than our vision. Avoiding the same mistakes they've made are their messages to us, we just have to take heed. Trying something new isn't so bad, especially if you've been receiving the same unsatisfactory results repeatedly.

Take note that starting with your mental must be put first. Your thoughts produce action, so whatever you keep on your mind, you will eventually do. Whether it's positive or negative thoughts, if it lingers around long enough, that thought will come to life. Once it comes to life, it'll turn into a habit and that habit may either be beneficial or it may cost you your life. So pay attention to what you're thinking about. If you're thinking about relocating with the same negative mentality, try again, but incorporate changing your way of thinking with your location, then you will be a powerful human being.

5

LESSONS UNLEARNED

"In school, you're taught a lesson and then given a test.
In life, you're given a test that teaches you a lesson."
-Tom Bodett

Out on bail with this new case only placed me in a situation of needing to get the money back that had been spent on bail, as well as cash to hire a lawyer. I still hadn't learned my lesson, and I was only getting myself involved in more illegal activity every time I was arrested. I needed money for my bills and to keep me from doing prison activity. Getting a job, at this point, wasn't going to provide me with the money I needed to continue my current way of living. I could've still pursued a job, but with my mentality, why would I do that? My constant run-ins with the police were the lessons I should've learned from, but I ignored the fact that it was me putting myself in these predicaments by choosing to continue making the same bad decisions. I continued looking for ways to outsmart the police and believed that they wouldn't catch me slipping the next time I had an encounter with them. As long as I continued to sell drugs, I would always have to look over my shoulders for the police. It's their job to catch me, and my job to not get caught. So far, I've been losing that battle and I still hadn't learned. Switching my location was my first step towards readjusting my criminal behavior. I couldn't remain in the same neighborhood I was arrested in because I would always be a target. Even if I wasn't doing anything, my reputation of being "up to no good" was going to continue to get me harassed by the officers. Being aware of this, I relocated to another neighborhood.

Having family that lived all over the city, gave me options on my next location. That mainly allowed me to have an address to use in case I was stopped by the police. I would be able to explain why I was in the neighborhood, and they wouldn't continue to focus on me. Knowing my face wasn't seen before, I would just say I was visiting my family, and they could vouch for me. I could sit on my family member's steps and not be bothered. That family member was my female cousin that I was partying with. Another cousin of mine lived two blocks away, and I was more than welcome at his place. Since I wasn't familiar with their neighborhood, I began observing how things operated before I jumped out there. I needed to be aware of the cops that were patrolling the area. Slowly, but surely, I had to slide my way into the drug activity. Luckily, I had some money saved up to pay my bills, because this process took about a month. When the time was right, I opened up shop just like before. I wasn't worried about getting rid of the product, I knew it would sell. Especially, since it was something new in the neighborhood. In the streets, the best product wins, but you still had to be consistent, because the drug addicts will go somewhere else if you don't have it. Always being equipped with the product was my goal. As long as I had drugs, money would always be coming in.

Unlike the last block I was on, this one pretty much was an open market. There wasn't anyone fully established on those corners like the other one. You had guys around hustling, but they weren't in one designated area. Certain drugs were either in bags or vials, and you were identified by the color of either one. If someone had the same color as yours, that would cause conflict, because the product is expected to be the same. Not wanting to get mixed up with anyone else, I made sure my colors were odd and never used. The product sold for itself, I didn't have to do much but wait for the addicts to come. As long as I was there, they would continue to come. A lot of times I stayed the night over my cousin's house, that way I could stay out late and come out early without having to go all the way home. I would just keep a change of clothes at his crib so I could refresh before I started the grind all over again. Things were back running smoothly, but I still had my court date to face.

As my court date arrived, my lawyer getting paid was a must. Before I entered the courthouse, I gave him another down payment. I was either expecting to get off completely or a postponement at my hearing since it was my initial hearing. With me believing that my case was weak, I chose a judge trial in District Court instead of sending it downtown to Circuit Court. It was my first arrest in Baltimore, so I didn't know any better. Plus, I was using my same lawyer that I hired for my arrest in Prince George's County, who wasn't a known attorney in the Baltimore Court system. The State ended up offering me a year in prison. At the time, I had no intentions of being away that long. I actually wasn't even thinking about going to prison for one day, so I declined. My refusal forced my case to go to trial right then in front of that judge. I still thought I would beat the case, because they found the gun in someone's yard after searching the area, not on my possession. However, the judge believed it to be mine and found me guilty of a simple handgun possession. I was sentenced to 18 months. Yet, all but six months were suspended. What was worse, I went to prison that exact same day. Since I was not prepared for that, I had to get my lawyer to make a phone call to my family to let them know what happened at court. I gave him my keys and all of my personal possessions to give to them as well. After ducking prison all those times throughout my entire time involved with the streets, it finally unexpectedly caught up to me.

Even though this wasn't my first time being locked up, I'd never been to prison before. I wouldn't say that I was scared, I just didn't know what to expect. Since this was my first prison sentence, and it was a short period of time for me to do, my security level was low. Therefore, I was sent to a minimum security prison. I never even left Baltimore City; the institution was actually right down the street from where I hung out. I had a six-month sentence, but as long as I stayed out of trouble, only about 3½ months would be required for me to serve. There were a few rules I had already discovered before going to prison, and if they were followed, I figured I'd make it through. The first rule was to mind my own business, because if not, I'd be asking for trouble. Number two was to never show any sign of weakness, so if I was to be tried, I had to immediately respond. Win, lose or draw would have to be the outcome, because if not, I knew I'd continue to be picked on. The last rule I vowed to myself, because I was a stand-up guy was that I would never join a gang. Avoiding trouble as much as possible was my focus, so being a part of a gang would've only placed me in situations that I didn't cause myself. Ensuring that I stuck by those three rules for the next few months of my life behind bars was critical.

Adapting to my environment was crucial as well. That is because things were run in order, and I had to go with the flow. From the telephone to the showers, you had to be aware of the rotation, because a sign of disrespect could possibly cost you your life. My cellmate, or "celly", was a lot older than me, so he gave me the run down on things. Due to him having spent almost a decade behind bars, he was well known and respected. That was a good thing, because I didn't have to worry about nonsense coming to my cell. Rain, sleet, or snow, we were provided with three meals, and we had to walk to the cafeteria to eat. Furthermore, we were allowed to purchase food from the commissary, so I made sure I had enough money on my books to get me through those few months. That helped out a lot, because the food wasn't anything like what I was used to. As a result of this, I would only go to certain meals.

Since the institution was minimum security, we could be out for recreation for most of the day. Yet, after each meal and during shift changes, we all had to lock in for count. When count cleared, we would either have courtyard, phone, showers, and dayroom privileges. I was good at basketball, so that was the recreation of choice at times for me. I also accumulated a few associates as a result of playing ball. Sports normally had that effect, especially when you had talent. Plus, me being in the streets, I knew some guys that were locked up. So by us all living the same type of lifestyle, prison was only predestined for us. Some just had more time than others. While staying active through the course of my incarceration, my release date came in no time. I was able to make it through without any trouble and altercations, and now I was prepared to head back home with the exact same plan in mind.

Although I didn't like being in prison, that experience wasn't enough for me to try something different. I viewed it as a cake walk, because I took the punishment without due consideration. Not seeing the real picture behind what was presented to me is the cause of me writing this book. The lesson that I was given was unlearned; though, it couldn't have been taught any better. I just wasn't ready to receive it at that time. See, I'm being taught the same exact lesson right now as I'm writing, I just finally decided to wake up. It took me experiencing time behind these walls on a few different occasions to finally get what was right before my eyes the entire time. That's why it's essential to learn from your past mistakes, because the more you continue to make them, the deeper and wider the hole becomes. Everyone receives lessons in life and those lessons shape our future. To make your future better than your past, learning from those lessons presented to you must be done the first time you encounter it. See, failure is a part of life, so don't be afraid to fail.

You can't have success without it; however, always use that failure to motivate yourself not to repeat the same mistakes. If you happen to repeat those mistakes like myself, don't let it keep you down, always get back up and never settle. Constantly keep in mind that failure is one of the most important lessons you can learn from, because you couldn't learn anything if your life was perfect.

6

CRIMINAL ADDICT

"What masters you, you won't let go,
What you've mastered, you'll let go."
-Unknown

Entering back into society with no plan was truly confirmation for more criminal activity to come. I didn't have anything positive on my mind, just thoughts of how can I do wrong much better than before without getting caught. I viewed the people I sold drugs to as addicts; yet, here I was an addict to the streets and crime. My addiction to criminal activity was expanding, as well as getting out of hand. The older I got, the more foolish I became. Through my previous run-ins with law enforcements, changing my perspective on my way of living should've been at the forefront of my mind. With that not being the case, I'm led to believe that at that moment in my life, I was an addict to criminal behavior. I will admit, like most addicts, I too was in denial about having a problem.

Generally, I was involved in selling drugs, but if there were any other schemes I could be a part of, I was willing to take the risk. Getting money was my focus. My mistake was that I was only looking at short term solutions, which caused me to be addicted to fast money. After being released from my short prison term, I picked up where I left off.

Not too much had changed while I was away for those few months; however, my money had gotten low. Needing to regroup, I just couldn't put myself in a situation to go right back to jail. Instead of going back to doing hand-to-hand transactions on the block, I gave someone else the work and just took a pay cut to remain off of the radar. Considering I still had to survive and pay my bills, I knew it was best to have less coming in than none at all. As long as I was able to receive the product, I would keep on pushing it. Something I'd learned at a young age was not to deal with any and every one. That was because it could lead to me getting ripped off by either copping a bad product or getting robbed. So when there were drug droughts, to avoid both of those predicaments, I would remain patient until I was able to deal with those I felt comfortable with.

Because I never knew what my life being involved in the streets would bring, saving was important. I was liable to be without product for weeks, maybe even months. Everybody involved in the drug game was at risk of being arrested. I say that because anything that's done illegally is an action that can risk one's loss of freedom, life, or what they have invested in. When I was in need of money, and the drugs weren't available, I adopted other hustles. While networking on other criminal activity to participate in, a friend of mine had a beneficial move for both of us.

After communicating with him, I learned that he had a hook-up on temporary vehicle tags I could sell. Since I was staying in Baltimore, it was the perfect location to get rid of them especially with the tags coming from Virginia. The price he was charging was so cheap so I was able to triple my money. Although I've never dealt with this type of hustle, I knew I'd still be able to get rid of them easily. The majority of the guys on the streets didn't have a driver's license, but they were still buying cars. Being able to purchase temporary vehicle tags meant that they were untraceable. That was a plus for them. All I needed to do was promote my merchandise, and what better way than to ride around on one of the tags myself. Once I sold tags to one person, they would just spread the word for me. Eventually, I had more customers than I could handle. Most of the time, they were sold before I even received a new bundle. Just like the drug game, there were times when I was on hold due to where they were initially coming from. The benefit to having those tags was the fact that I was able to receive other things to make a profit off of. They were very valuable to a lot of individuals, which resulted in me getting some of the most irresistible offers. This hustle seemed to be much less of a risk than selling drugs; however, it only elevated my criminal addiction. Nevertheless, like with any good hustle, it also eventually came to an end.

Losing the hook-up on the tags caused me to go back to what I knew the most, selling drugs. Networking with all the new people I dealt with from the vehicle tag hustle, opened more doors for me to be in a position to sell any illegal merchandise that I was able to get my hands on. When one type of criminal activity has taken place in a person's life, others involved are more than likely caught up in other crimes as well. The more options I had, the better I saw my state of affairs. With my options limited, it was back to selling drugs in the hood.

Not being on the block every day like I was before the vehicle tag hustle, I wasn't aware of the new faces in the area. The same way I had family in the area when I started making my move, it wasn't any different for any other individuals. As far as I was concerned, they weren't going to interfere with what I had going on. I was good at marketing my product, and my product was considered top shelf and always different than my competition. Their product was coming from a different source. Having that advantage of something different allowed my product to sell much quicker. Faced with jealousy and envy in the streets, complications were soon to occur.

As I continued my daily routine, I was approached by one of the guys. Due to their money flow slowing up, they felt like they needed to get me from around the vicinity. Not even knowing me, one guy said, "*No disrespect, dudes don't want you around here.*" Unafraid of any type of conflict, I told him I didn't understand the problem and that it was enough money for everyone. He insisted on me leaving the area, and I did, but with a mind frame of going to war. After discussing the matter with my cousins, the situation was resolved considering that they knew the guys. Before any violence could occur, the beef was squashed. I stayed in the area for a little while longer, but shortly after, a better proposition came my way.

Up until moving back to Baltimore, the drugs I'd always sold were either crack cocaine or marijuana. I did get to see how heroin shops were running in a very organized manner. I even participated in one of the shops when I first arrived. I got on my feet by doing so, but afterwards, I went back to what I was more familiar with, which was cocaine and marijuana. Although I was familiar with heroin, I didn't know the exact procedure for mixing that particular drug.

A family member, who was in a great position in the drug game gave me an opportunity to make some real cash. I was taught the mixing process, as well as how to cap the heroin for sale. After packaging the drugs, I would just give the package to the guys that were running their blocks. Since the system was well organized, I didn't have to do much but have the product ready when they ran low. With me having more than one person I was distributing to, it simply allowed me to bring in more money. This didn't require too much of my time, because they would have enough product to last the entire day. It was kind of a predictable cash flow for each block, so my schedule was pretty much free.

The money I was bringing in was better than I've ever experienced, particularly since it was all profit. I was getting paid a large amount of cash for doing pretty much nothing. Never being satisfied with enough money, I continued to distribute drugs to some of my peers in the neighborhood I was hustling in. Bringing in this kind of cash and having so much free time was the reason I ended up spending a lot of money. I was able to buy pretty much anything I wanted, and if I wanted it, I would get it. A large amount of my time was spent shopping and eating at the best restaurants. Sometimes after the heroin shops were shut down, me and my friends would link up and go to NBA games or different clubs to enjoy ourselves. Being involved in this kind of operation, I just knew I would be selling drugs my entire life. With no interaction with police officers, I felt untouchable. The biggest risk I was taking was driving with drugs in my car. With me having my driver's license and traveling alone, I felt I could handle the police if I was pulled over. Never being faced with that situation, merely allowed me to remain comfortable within my criminal activity. My addiction for dealing drugs, as well as my free time, led me back into the original neighborhoods where I started selling drugs, which was a bad move. With me being back in my comfort zone, it wasn't long before trouble had come my way.

With the operation running well, I didn't necessarily need to be around the neighborhood, but being addicted to all the action that came with the street life, I was lured in. My thoughts were, *if I'm going to hang around, why not sell the drugs as well.* Financially, I was in a position to where I could stand a loss and I was able to give

guys better deals than what they could receive from someone else. .
At times, the block was "extremely hot", meaning the police stayed in
the area. Everybody on the block was known for selling drugs but
not getting caught with them on or near you was the task. If someone
was told not to be seen by an officer and that order was violated, one
was probably going to be hauled off to jail for loitering or a dirty cop
might result to planting drugs on someone for disobeying their order.
Knowing it was risky to play with the cops, a lot of guys would just
disappear for the day and others, would try to maneuver around
them.

With this taking place, one particular day I ended up giving some
product to someone I normally wouldn't deal with. I did know the
guy from his relationship with my nephew's mother, and he had his
own thing going on, but not at this time. Since I had the best deals
around, he couldn't refuse, because it was easy money for him. After
dealing with him a few times, he decided to play games with my
money by not giving me what he owed me. I never would ask him for
the money, he would always say he "got me" whenever he saw me.
Tired of him continuing to drag me on about my money, I asked him
about his plans on paying me. He aggressively expressed to me, "*I got
you, and don't press up on me about the money!*" Not taking that response
too kindly, and without a reply, I banged him in his mouth. We
fought for a few minutes until it was broken up. Not wanting to be
arrested, my friend and I headed to the car and left.

After this fight took place, it was a rumor that he was jumped by
me and a few others, when in all reality, we were fighting one-on-one
the entire time. Even though I got the best of him, he did get one
good punch in and blackened my eye. I was mad about that, but even
madder for him lying about the fight. I took the money he owed me
as a loss and just chalked it up. It was viewed as part of the game.
Knowing that I should've never dealt with him in the first place, was
the lesson that I had learned. Continuing my daily routines, one
afternoon I was called about my nephew's house being raided by the
police and that they were looking for me. I was shocked, because I
only visited his home. I wasn't doing any drug activity there.
Gathering my thoughts, I knew exactly where it had come from.
Since the police were given my license plate number, a description of
my car and I'd been identified as having a gun, I immediately traded

my car for a newer one. Not wanting to get caught up once again, at the time, changing my ride was my best move. Unfortunately, that wasn't enough, because it wasn't long after the previous house raid, that I was located, watched, chased, and once again arrested.

When hearing the word addict, the thoughts of being hooked on drugs or considered a junky comes to mind more often than not. The definition of the word addict is: **To devote or surrender (oneself) to something habitually or obsessively, which leaves the door open for a variety of things.** In life, you have people that are addicted to sex, gambling, drugs, food, coffee, alcohol, fashion, money, etc. Criminal activity was my addiction. I was unaware that my criminal mentality was expanding each and every time I got away with a crime. If I happen to get caught, I would only blame it on someone else, never holding myself accountable for my actions.

Being in denial is very dangerous for a person. They will continue to fault others for what has happened to them and not themselves. Having the courage to admit when you are wrong is one attribute you most want to inherit. As long as you remain in denial for whatever you're up against, whatever place you are in – you shall remain.

7

CHOSEN ADVERSITY

"We choose our joys & sorrows long
before we experience them."
-Khalil Gibran

Getting arrested wasn't new to me, but not knowing what I was charged with bothered me. When I was being transported in the police van to central booking, my mind was racing on what I could've done. I didn't get arrested for anything and not appear in court for it. And when my nephew's house was raided, I wasn't there, and I didn't even live there, so if anything was found, it couldn't have linked back to me. As I was being watched, the house I was seen coming out of was searched by the police, but whatever they were arresting me for had nothing to do with that house. Confused after seeing the Commissioner, I found out I was being charged with 1st degree attempted murder, and was given no bail. What made matters worse; I ended up getting re-booked for an armed robbery charge as well. With having no bail on two charges, I knew I was faced with a serious dilemma. My only hope at this time was to get my charges reduced or hear the words "No Bail" changed to some kind of monetary bail, which was also denied by the judge at my bail hearing.

At the time of my arrest, I didn't know who the victim was. I didn't even know this guy's name, and I know he didn't know mine, so I couldn't figure out how my name was ever mentioned. After I was able to read the police report, I figured out who the person was because of the neighborhood where the shooting took place; he was from that area. I eventually found out that he identified me out of a photo line-up. Though we did have an altercation once before, me shooting him never took place. Come to find out, that's why my nephew's home was raided. When you're viewed as a threat, people will do any and everything to get you out of the way. As far as the robbery charge, I was framed for robbing a lady for $35 in a neighborhood I wasn't even aware of. All I could think of was the cops framing me because they knew the attempted murder charge was phony, and with an additional violent offense, I would just have to go through the whole waiting process to prove my innocence. I was labeled as a gun carrier, but robbery wasn't in my character at all. However, I was faced with two violent crimes and it didn't look good for me. Since I didn't receive bail, getting a great lawyer was all I could rely on. After about a week, my cousin sent a lawyer to speak with me. After our conversation, I immediately knew I would be sitting for a while.

Not having bail meant I would be moving from Central Booking to Baltimore City jail. Since this was my first time in the detention center, I didn't know what to expect. I knew what prison was like from my first experience, but this was not as privileged. You were supposed to be considered innocent until proven guilty, but that for sure wasn't the case. We were in our cells for 20 hours a day, and were able to come out for only four hours! During that break, we showered, used the phone and played some sort of cards. On certain days, we were given gym or outside courtyard for approximately one hour, which may have cut into our normal time out of our cells. A lot of times those privileges were taken due to the amount of violence taking place on the cellblock. They would keep us secluded as much as possible to avoid having to keep us locked down. Keeping the violence down as much as possible was the only solution. It was impossible for it to be none at all because there were too many ongoing beefs from the streets, as well as too many different personalities all in one confined location. You had some individuals that didn't have people on the outside looking out for them, so if you had something they wanted and you were considered weak, that was another problem you were faced with. Going through this on a daily basis would stretch any person thin, so being mentally strong was the only way to survive.

The living space we were in was extremely small; it was like living in a small bathroom. Then to be sharing that space with another grown man only made matters worse. The fact that it probably was a total stranger added more stress. Everything from meals to leisure most often happened in the cell. I hated how our food was passed to us through a slot. And talk about no privacy! When I had to defecate, it had to be done right in the cell with my roommate. The way we showed respect during times like that is by using a sheet to make a curtain to divide the tiny space. On commissary day, which is the day that we receive ordered goods, I would have to reach through the same slot that was used to pass our meals to us to grab my belongings, all while still locked in. We were, however, able to receive Walkman radios and cassette tapes with our initial package. The music helped me cope with the circumstances and it blocked a lot of noise on the tier.

With the city jail being so overcrowded, the court docket was always considered backed up, which was caused by numerous postponements. The system was set up to force inmates to either accept a plea deal or remain at the detention center to await trial. Since I wasn't willing to take any sort of deal, I sat and received one trial postponement after another. Due to my case being prolonged for close to two years, I experienced some difficult times as each season changed. The winter and summer months were the most detrimental times I've ever experienced in my entire life. Having to choose from the two, I would pick the winter over the summer any day.

Each tier had a cat walk with windows right in front of our cells. By the jail being so beat down, you had broken windows that were open all year round. During the winter months, this allowed all of the cold air to come right in on the tier. With the cells having bars, you felt every bit of the low temperature. Sleeping with all my clothes on was a must to stay warm. If I was able to get trash bags, I'd tie them on my grill, which was the feeding slot on my door, to block out as much of the cold air as possible. While I hated those conditions, I'd much rather it than the summer months. The summer heat was straight torture. Even with a breeze, the windows were at a distance, so I really never felt the breeze anyway. They put two fans on each tier to blow from the back of the unit to the front, but it was all hot air. So not having the fan blow directly on me with cool air meant I was constantly sweating. To try to enjoy some kind of breeze, I'd stick cardboard through my grill to get some of the air from the fan.

That was a technique most of us used to try to stay a little cool. I could barely get any sleep, and when I did, I would wake up with my sheets soaked from sweating. The times we received ice were like moments from heaven. This lasted for a short period of time, but I enjoyed every single cube that was in my cup.

The seasons also determined the temperature of the water. It was either freezing cold or scalding hot. Putting up with the water being cold in the winter and hot in the summer was extremely frustrating. Mental toughness was honestly the only thing that got me through these abnormal conditions. Watching guys over a period of time let the circumstances get the best of them, such as pleading guilty although they may have been innocent of a crime, attempting suicide, or going mentally insane, only pushed me harder to remain strong. Knowing that I was going to continue to plead not guilty, I didn't know how long my stay would be at the city jail, so I did whatever I could to cope with my conditions.

Everyone incarcerated was accused of breaking the law, so being behind bars wouldn't stop a person with a criminal mentality. With the help of correctional officers, cigarettes, marijuana, and other things were available in the jail. Even though I hated cigarettes, there was a time when I couldn't get my hands on any weed, so I'd just smoke tobacco. I didn't smoke tobacco regularly; at times, it was just something I did to cope with my situation. Remaining high only made me ignore the pain and suffering I was up against, but once the high went away, reality always kicked back in.

On days when we had to go to court, we had to get up around 3:30AM just to go sit in a crowded bull pen to wait to get searched, shackled, and transported to the court house. Although we were up that early, we never left the jail before 8:00AM, because the court house was less than 10 minutes away. Being frustrated was an understatement because we went through this whole process for every court appearance. Not to mention that it was even more stressful when we went through all of that to spend no longer than 10 minutes in the courtroom, only to receive a postponement. This process only discouraged me more for having to go back to the city jail to wait for another 90-120 days to do it all over again. Actually, this process could break anyone and it was the reason so many people took just any kind of plea deal. With me having a **Never Give**

In & Never Give Up mentality, I remained strong until I finally reached my official trial date.

When it came to my trial, I can admit it was really scary for me. My life was on the line and if found guilty of the charges, I was facing the rest of my life in prison. Having no other choice but to go all the way, I picked the jury and allowed my attorney to argue my case. I was on trial for the attempted murder charge, so in order to convict me; the jury would have to believe the evidence that was brought against me. With no evidence, and the victim's story not matching the original police report, my trial didn't last long and the jury found me not guilty. The same day, the robbery trial had supposedly taken place, but due to the victim not showing up for the trial, the state nolle prossed the case, and I was released the next day.

My experience at the detention center was the worst ever, but it still didn't deter me from the lifestyle. My mentality stayed the same, and I left the jail with no plans or goals to do anything different from before. I still remember walking out of those doors, forgetting everything that I had just gone through. To a person outside looking in, they would say I was crazy. Looking back on my life and knowing what I know now, I would just say I was lost. That's why it's important to surround yourself around those that will help you grow and push you to do better.

You have a choice in life, so let the choices you make today, be the ones you can live with tomorrow. Whatever you decide, that will determine how your future turns out. So, in order for you to have a bright future, choose wisely and think before you act.

8

RELUCTANT TO CHANGE

"If nothing changes, nothing changes."
-Unknown

With the most horrible experience I've ever encountered behind me, I still chose the same lifestyle that forced me to face all that I had went through. I still hadn't learned my lesson, and truly wasn't seeing that I was only back pedaling in life. Expected to do something different was impossible. My thought process stayed the same even under those hideous circumstances. Given that I had access to marijuana at the jail, I brought that habit home with me. When I was released after fighting for my life, one of the first things I did was get high. Having an unclear mind is never good; you only allow your judgment to be cloudy. In the world we live in, you must be a thinker. Without using your ability to think wisely, you will continue to repeat your mistakes. Since I was reluctant to change that meant the company I kept was involved in the same thing I was yearning for. So once I arrived back home, I received money to hold me over until I actually went back to dealing drugs again. Most guys would rather give you drugs, and let you make your own money, than offer you money to give you a head start. By no means was I going to continue to keep receiving handouts. Therefore, I was given my own drugs to put in my own work and get my own money.

When I was released from the jail, I was once again able to be liberated from the judicial system all together. However, two months after being out, my lawyer called to explain to me that the State's Attorney had reopened the robbery case. I didn't understand how that was possible but now I'm back faced with another probability of going back to prison. What made it a little easier on me was the fact that my lawyer had worked it out where I was able to fight the case while still being on the streets. Having the same attitude, I was going to try and get as much money and have as much fun as possible just in case I had to go to prison. There weren't any guarantees when involved in the street life, and even though I didn't commit the crime that they were charging me with, they were still trying to send me away for it. What baffled me the most was my picture being shown to this woman in the first place. This was a real concern since I'd never been arrested for a robbery charge in my life. Furthermore, the area the incident took place in, was an area I didn't even know anything about, including where it was. I hadn't ever even had any run-ins with the police in that area. My main problem was proving my innocence to the judge and the jury; especially when someone identified me as the suspect. With all these thoughts coming to mind, prolonging my court date as long as possible was all I could come up with.

Already being established in a variety of neighborhoods, I just chose one that I felt the most comfortable in to start selling drugs again. I figured I was smarter by not doing the hand-to-hand transactions myself and just sitting out on the block watching everything get sold. Riding with the drugs wasn't as risky to me as it was being watched on the block by the knockers (plain clothes police). It wasn't like I would be riding around with them all day; I would take them to their destination and drop them off. Just like riding with the narcotics, having large amounts of money on me was no different. If the cops were to pull me over and my car was searched, I would potentially have to explain where the large sum of cash came from, and then hope they wouldn't take it from me. I wasn't expecting to meet head-on with this reality, but surely I would in time, and the turnout was more unpleasant than I expected.

One evening, while riding with a friend, I drove by the police who decided to pull us over and mess with us. I wasn't doing anything illegal, so they had no reason to pull us over. Though I didn't have anything illegal in the car, I did have a large sum of money, but I still didn't' have a problem with being pulled over. Since I had my driver's license and the car was registered properly, I didn't feel that there was any need to search the vehicle. With that not being the case, I had to think fast on explaining where the money had come from. Therefore,

I told them I'd just sold a car and was going to go purchase another one. The officers didn't buy the story so they just searched the car extra hard for drugs. While they searched the vehicle, they had us sitting on the curb in handcuffs. About 30 minutes later, a tow truck and a police wagon pulled up and they sent us to jail. While I'm asking what we were getting locked up for, one officer said, "*For selling drugs.*" My friend and I were heated, but it was nothing we could do about it. We took the ride to central bookings to appear in front of the commissioner.

After receiving my charging documents, the officers put in the report that we had a big bag of dope in the car along with the money recovered. I thought that they may have taken some of the money for their own personal use, but they hadn't. They placed the entire amount found within the charging documents. That was surprising to me because we didn't have any drugs at all, so for them to lie about the amount of cash found instead of lying about the drugs seemed more fitting for their actions. This caused a major setback for me. Once again, I was given no bail. After losing the cash I had on me, I had to spend more money on a lawyer to get a monetary bail, and then spend more money to pay the bail to get out. All of this took place within the span of 60 days. Now I was back out on the streets with the goal of getting the money that was lost and spent back.

Each time I was released, I felt I had to make up for what was lost, and though this thought process was not logically working for me, it still didn't make me want to change the way I did things. I was in too deep! The only thing I could see was the life I was living. It was crazy, but I had tunnel vision. If I was to stop, how would I survive, I kept asking myself? No sound answer came to mind; therefore, I only saw things one way. I thought I was supposed to continue hustling in order to live on. I was pretty much trapped, because if I didn't continue to sell drugs, the money I needed for bills, lawyers, and bail wouldn't be available. As long as I continued to be out there, I risked going back to jail every day. Realistically, for me, this was a lose-lose situation and I had no one to blame but myself. I created the conditions I was in with my poor decision making. In view of the fact that I continued to live life on the edge, my fate continued to be behind bars. A month after bailing out, I was rearrested for another handgun charge, and I knew I wasn't going to receive another opportunity to bail out. Therefore, getting prepared to do time was my next move.

In the midst of these different cases pending all at one time, I believed I was going to get some prison time but how much was the question. Out of the three charges, I was only guilty of having the handgun. Proving my innocence on the other two charges was the concern. Since the robbery charge was a couple of years old, the trial date was already scheduled. While my time to appear in court had come, mentally, I wasn't prepared to go to trial. Unfortunately, my attorney was prepared, but after talking to the State's Attorney, he was able to work a deal for all three charges. Initially, I refused to plead guilty to a crime I didn't commit. I didn't want an armed robbery charge on my record, especially knowing I was innocent and it would hinder me later on down the line. The drug charge was a lie as well, but I considered that conviction especially since I sold drugs; I just hadn't been caught with any. After a conversation with my mom, and considering all three charges getting resolved at one time, I decided to take the plea deal of 12 years in prison, with all suspended but 6 years.

With the armed robbery case being a couple years back, the two years I sat fighting the case over in the city jail was credited to me. As a result, I originally had two years already in on the six-year sentence. Knowing that I didn't have to do my entire sentence, my mindset still hadn't quite changed. Even though I didn't want to go to prison, I took my punishment, because I saw the light at the end of the tunnel. I knew I wouldn't be behind those walls any longer than another three years as long as I didn't get into any trouble. Still being reluctant to change, I wasn't ready to learn from what I was going to experience.

In order to change, it has to start from within. No matter what you go through and how bad you may not like your conditions, if the changes don't start from within, things will always remain the same. I'm speaking from experience, because my unwillingness to transform my mentality only resulted in me getting a lengthy prison sentence. Having new priorities were needed in my life, because not understanding that the old way would never measure up to the actual desires for my life was causing more harm for me as well as others. When you continue to make the same dreadful choices, it makes it hard for those to believe in you when you really do decide to change.

Nevertheless, don't let that discourage you from continuing to do better. You have to remember that your constant poor decision-making has opened the door for those to perceive you as a constant failure. Let their perception of you be your motivation to prove them wrong and demonstrate through your actions that people do change and we all are a work-in-progress. No matter how many times you fall, always get back up. Understand that in order to change your conditions, you must change your vision.

9

WASTED OPPORTUNITY

"The greatest waste in the world is the difference between what we are & what we could become."
-Ben Herbster

Taking the plea bargain was one of the most important decisions I've ever made in my entire life. It was difficult, because admitting guilt for something I didn't do bothered me. However, the judge told me if I had lost my case, he was going to give me 40 years. So, to receive the sentence of six years for all three charges was only another opportunity for me to change my mindset. Yeah, I was going to prison to do more time than I had before, but I also knew that I wasn't facing life behind bars or just a longer period of time like others that I knew.

In fact, at this time I had an uncle that was incarcerated for approximately 40 years for a crime that he did not commit, and he was still fighting to prove his innocence. The time that my uncle spent behind bars could never be given back; however, how he used his time is really what counts.

Now that I had the opportunity to change my way of thinking, I used some of the resources available to better myself, but it was only so I could get home quicker. I didn't have a well thought out plan of what I was going to do once I was released. My mind wasn't focused on doing the same things like before, but I didn't prepare for the reality I was going to be facing when I completed my sentence. So with another trip to prison, it turned out to be an opportunity wasted, instead of one used to my advantage.

Familiar with the penal system, I already knew how to survive under the circumstances. The same rules that I applied throughout my first appearance, were to be followed wherever I was sent. With the length of my prison sentence plus time credited, my security level should've been minimum, but the nature of the charges caused my points to be a little higher and pushed me into a medium institution in Hagerstown, Maryland. The city jail and prison were different in various ways, mainly because in prison men respect men. Given the fact that there are men living there for the rest of their lives, it's a lot more structure and less nonsense. That's why my focus going in was to do my time and to get back home.

Even behind the prison walls, I had opportunities to sharpen myself up; it all depended on how I used my time. I had to be eligible for certain jobs and shops that were available within the institution. After seeing the case manager and letting them know what job I preferred, they placed me on the waiting list until a spot was open. School was mandatory for anyone who didn't have their G.E.D. or High School Diploma. Given that I graduated high school, getting a copy of my diploma sent in to verify my completion was mandatory to avoid going to school. Once I received the copy, it was placed in my file and the case manager placed me in for a vocational shop.

H.V.A.C. (Heating Ventilation & Air Conditioning) was my trade of choice. The need of heat and air conditioning would always be a necessity, so I figured I couldn't go wrong with learning the basics. Classes were Monday through Friday, which required book work and hands-on projects. Although, the teacher I had was cool, he wasn't a real big help. The things I learned in class actually came from one of my classmates who was familiar with the course. It was his line of work while he was on the streets. I was willing to learn all that I could, but my main reason for taking the shop was to earn 10 extra days off of my sentence each month. As long as I was working or in school, I could earn good conduct credits, as well as state pay, which was based on the type of job I held. Certain jobs paid more than others, but I was more concerned with knocking my release date down than the money. With that being my focus, I didn't take the opportunity to learn the trade as efficiently as I should have. Having the opportunity to really educate myself was wasted on frivolous thinking. I was just trying to get by and not ahead. There was a test at the end of the class that would have given me a certification in the trade and made it possible for me to deal with different types of refrigerants.

Even though I didn't take the class seriously, due to my lack of studying, I still received a Type 1 Certification. If I would have taken advantage of this opportunity, I could've gotten my Universal License, and been accessible for a number of jobs. Not thinking that far ahead, I was content with what I had accomplished.

Upon completing the course, I continued to stay in the shop for as long as I could in order to continue receiving those extra days. Eventually, I was removed from the class and transferred to another facility as a result of my security level dropping to minimum. My time was getting shorter, so when I went for my yearly review with my case manager, I requested to move to an institution closer to my home. I knew by letting her know I was trying to participate in the Occupational Skills & Training Center (O.S.T.C.) Program, I had a great chance of getting back into the city limits. Therefore, I was placed on the waiting list and transferred as soon as an opening became available.

Each facility had their benefits. Being in Hagerstown, the food was better and the staff didn't have a problem responding to requests, such as signing up for programs and referring an inmate for a job. While in the city, the food was awful and I barely got to see my case manager. However, I was closer to home and had more access to contraband. Since I wasn't preparing for my transition home, the closer I got to being released, the more lax I became. Yep, I got sucked right back into criminal activity, and was about to risk losing everything I'd worked hard for. After arriving in the city facility, I fell right back into my old behavior.

To understand the process for being able to go to a minimum security facility, you had to be close to going home and free of infractions for at least a year, if not more. Once in the camp, any ticket or infraction caused security levels to increase. With having access to all types of contraband, if you didn't have any self-discipline, you would end right up in the mix. Risking additional charges and getting sent back to a medium security institution happened often. Not tired of making poor decisions, I got caught up in the mix just like everyone else. As a result of being well connected, it made it easier for me to get my hands on the things I wanted. Not long after my arrival, I was able to acquire a cell phone and weed was at my discretion until I finished doing the rest of my time. Fortunately, I didn't get caught with any contraband, so I escaped any inconvenient moving. There was a time I came close to receiving a positive test result for drugs, or a "dirty urine". I was randomly picked for a urinalysis test, and from smoking weed on a regular, I was for sure going to fail. After using someone else's urine in place of mine, I was able to get over that hurdle. What's even crazier is that I continued to smoke as if being released at that time wasn't at risk.

After being in the facility for a few months, I started the O.S.T.C. Program. From my interest in and experience with cars, I chose to participate in the automotive shop and I actually looked forward to going to class. The book work was really boring but I had the opportunity to work on some of the cars in the shop and I almost forgot that I was still locked up. I became cool with a few of the guys in the class and we made the best out of our conditions. Even though we had fun in the class, we weren't putting our heads together to try and use the skills we were learning when we were released. Having the opportunity to receive all the information we had for free, I clearly failed to use what I learned to my advantage. People pay to learn what we were being taught for free and here I'd taken it for granted. I did great in class and was able to have some of my family members come see me graduate, but I still didn't take the accomplishment as serious as I should have. It was just part of the process for me to get home. Like in my past, I still didn't have any plans or goals once I appeared back in society. I figured I'd just take life however it came. Of course the odds were already against me, so this was the wrong approach, especially after doing time in prison. Without appropriate grounding, I wasn't going to truly be able to handle the challenges I would soon face.

As I got closer to my release date, 90 days before my mandatory date, I was eligible for home monitoring. My plan for discharge was to use my godmother's address, so I had to make sure everything was in order for me to be released. Once the officers visited my home and the house was considered suitable for me to be released to, I knew I'd be leaving any day. I just didn't know the actual day because of security reasons. So I patiently waited to be called upon to pack up. When the day finally arrived, I was able to have a small pre-taste of freedom. Though being on the box was still considered incarceration and I couldn't leave the house unless I was scheduled to see my agent, I was happy to be in a position to eat home cooked meals. I also liked being able to receive visits at any given time. With only about 45 days on the box, before I knew it, I was free again. I was assigned probation, and still required to follow a few stipulations. I was able to go and come as I pleased, and without having anything lined up for employment, networking to find a job was my next move.

Prison wasn't any place I wanted to be, however, those vocational shops were opportunities of a lifetime. If I had only taken them seriously, I could've had a career in one of those fields. Yet by me wasting those opportunities, I wasn't near as prepared to legally survive once I was released back into society. I was clueless on where I was going to look for a job. Also, the time I spent smoking marijuana and worried about things of no benefit was actually the time that I needed to strategize on some form of employment and a legal way to survive out in the real world.

See, using your time wisely is very important, because time moves forward, not backwards. Getting back the time I wasted is impossible, so I want to encourage you to make the best of your present. When you have the opportunity to progress and learn something new, take advantage of those times. Trust and believe someone else would love to be in your shoes. Everyone's situation is different and you can't predict how your tomorrow will be. Let taking advantage of your today be at the top of the list. It's nothing worse than looking back over time and wishing you had done or used something that was beneficial for your future.

In order to remain on course, don't waste your time and don't let anyone else waste your time. Always ask yourself, what you are doing with your time to prepare for your future. If it's nothing productive, know that you're wasting your life and an opportunity to become great.

10

RUNNING FROM THE CHALLENGE

"The ultimate measure of a man is not where he stands in moments
of comfort and convenience, but where he
stands at times of challenge and controversy."
-Dr. Martin Luther King Jr.

Looking for employment was my primary focus. It was a blessing that I had support, so I had a few dollars to hold me over. However, no one was going to keep helping me if I wasn't willing to help myself. Plus, I wasn't the type who didn't want to work or get my own, so I started networking to find job opportunities. I even went to different career centers that helped ex-offenders. As soon as I was taken off of home monitoring, I immediately went to the Maryland Motor Vehicle Administration (MVA) to renew my driver's license. I've always kept them intact, so having my license was a big help towards receiving employment. It also allowed me to drive family and friends vehicles until I was able to get my own. My older sister had a car she wasn't driving, so she let me borrow her vehicle until I got myself together. All I had to do was put some air in the tires and I was ready to go. A few weeks later, a friend of mine gave me a pick-up truck that he had sitting around. It needed to be inspected and registered with liability insurance, so I couldn't drive it right away. Also, due to the truck being old, it was in need of a tune-up. I reached out to a few people and received help with getting the truck on the road. Timing was perfect, because shortly after getting the truck together, I received a call for a job.

The employer wanted to interview me and offer me a temporary position at the Port of Baltimore. My job description was to place labels on the trucks & cars. Since I had my license, I was also able to move and park the company vehicles in the parking lot. Knowing how to drive a stick shift also placed me in a better position than the average employee. After my interview, I was asked to start working the next day. My work hours were from 6:30PM until 12:30AM. I made sure I was always on time, and by the end of my 90 day probationary period, I was recognized by my boss for doing a great job. He also gave me a raise. Although the pay wasn't all that great, getting paid weekly helped out enormously. The work wasn't hard either, so I didn't feel like I was slaving for pennies. After selling drugs for so many years, I actually felt good about making money the honest way and not having to look over my shoulder.

By staying with my godmother, I didn't have any serious bills. I would just help her with a few of her bills and groceries. By showing effort in doing something positive, I was receiving blessings along the way. After working for a while and with a steady routine, eventually I was laid off. It wasn't due to anything dealing with my work ethic, but lack of work on the company's behalf. Once again, I was in need of a job.

Networking was my strength and another job opportunity came up. My brother spoke with his friend's wife who was working at *One Stop Auto*. After speaking with her and giving her my experience in the automotive field, she secured me an interview and I was hired on the spot. Again, having my driver's license was beneficial. I mainly cleaned up around the shop but I was also sent out to pick up other cars from different dealerships they were partnered with. This job was paying a little more than the last job, as well as weekly. Plus, I had a permanent position. The work wasn't complicated at all, but at times it was rather slow and boring. When it wasn't busy, I would try to keep myself occupied. However, there were times where there just wasn't anything for me to do.

Not wanting to be seen sitting around, I would go sit in one of the vehicles and one of my co-workers would let me know if the boss was coming. It was a few times I was caught sitting around doing nothing and the boss told me I needed to be working. I knew letting him know that there wasn't anything for me to do wasn't a good idea. So to look busy, I grabbed a broom and started sweeping. It seemed as if he wanted to pick with me because he was aware of when the shop was slow on business. However, I did my best to avoid conflicts.

One day, I was asked to move the vehicles that were parked across the street back to the dealership's lot. As I was about to cross the street, I was called back and told I wasn't moving fast enough. Not wanting to be disrespectful, I asked him what he meant by that. He told me I needed to put some "pep in my step" or run when asked to do something. Unfamiliar with being spoken too in this manner, other than by my mother as a child, I immediately gave him a peace of my mind. He implied that I either do what he says, or leave. I humbly left the premises before the situation got out of hand. I'm not sure if I was just being tested or what, but I wasn't sticking around to find out. Unable to accept being spoken to in that manner, I only returned back to the job site to pick up my check. Although, I quit the job, I felt that was the best thing for me at the time. Staying there would have only allowed the situation to become worse and it may have even gotten me sent back to prison. Unsure of what I was going to do next, I ended up right back around the same neighborhoods that I was known to sell drugs in.

Leaving the job was unexpected, and I wasn't prepared for the unknown. Being challenged by my boss had only placed me in the mindset of not needing to answer to anyone. Instead of going out to search for another job, I never gave myself a chance and took the easy way out. See, I was uncomfortable when I was faced with that type of conflict, and instead of facing it, I just ran away from it. I ended up making excuses, telling myself that I wasn't getting paid enough money anyway. Clearly aware of the fact that I could make my weekly pay in a day's time, I dismissed everything that I'd been through in the past from getting fast money. Once my mind was made up on going back to the streets, I no longer even thought about working for someone else.

Part of my probation requirements were either to have a job or go to school. As for everything else, my agent wasn't having any issues with me. I always reported on my scheduled appointment dates, and my urinalysis test were always clean. After a year of this consistent behavior, my level was reduced to fewer appointments. When it came to my employment status, I would just say I was working under the table, looking for something better. As long as I didn't have any new arrests, I was alright. At this time, I wasn't on the scene with my drug activity, so my chances of getting caught weren't as high. There were times when I would help out a friend of mine with side jobs dealing with home improvement work too. That worked out because with me having the pick-up truck, I could haul trash to the dump for him and scrap metal to the scrap yard. Doing some actual work and not being seen in one spot all day long made me feel like I wouldn't be recognized as one of the well-known drug dealers. Having that as my way of thinking, I would just appear in different neighborhoods all over the city throughout the day.

Even with being back out in the streets, at times, I still tried to do some positive things. With a creative mind, a buddy of mine and I were talking about starting a car wash. The location was going to be in his neighborhood, but we needed a power washing machine. In the company of different people that I dealt with, I shortly came across an associate who had and was willing to sell his for a little to nothing. I bought it with no hesitation and called my buddy to let him know that we were a step closer to executing our plan. After getting all of the necessary equipment, my nephew's older cousin, who was well experienced with detailing vehicles, came to help us out and we started our business with a small clientele. The majority of our customers were family and friends who wanted to support us. Eventually, business picked up a little more. When we became very busy, I would pitch in and help out as well. It was important for me to show my worker that I had no problem helping out. Always trying to make a dollar, another opportunity and idea that offered more income came up.

A friend of mine had a smoke grill she was trying to get rid of. Instead of me getting rid of it, I thought it would be a great idea to sell dinners at the car wash. I was confident with the idea because I knew as long as the food was good, it would sell, especially while people were waiting for their cars to get clean. So I brought the grill over to the car wash and discussed my idea with my partner. Our next step was figuring out what food we were going to sell. The meat was taken care of due to my friend working at a meat factory. He was able to give it to us using his discount. I had my aunt, cousins, and female friends cook the sides for me and my brother and I would grill the meat. With all the utensils to keep the food warm, platters were ready to go for $10 a plate. It turned out to be a great move, because the food was good and people that weren't getting their car washed bought plates too. The business was starting to do well, but due to poor judgment, it was eventually shut down.

Selling drugs always causes some sort of problems and trying to mix that with what we had going on at the car wash was a bad idea. The decision to keep the drug activity so close to the car wash seemed rational at the time. Whether I had my own drugs or not, they were still going to be sold in the area. If I would've just kept this particular spot clean with drug activity on my behalf, the shutdown would have never taken place. See, the property we were located on was owned by a drug user that I sold to and giving this person drugs eventually slapped me in the face. No one was arrested or anything, it was just a misunderstanding involving some money. With the business not lasting long, I was back to selling drugs full time all over again.

As I continued to remain in the drug game, I had a few people trying to get me out of the streets. With so much free time on my hands, I ended up going back and forth to the car auction with a friend of mine. Watching how he was spending his time and investing his money legally to make more was pretty interesting. He asked me on several occasions to leave the streets alone and come mess with his legit hustle. With me being comfortable with what I was doing, I was willing to give it a shot, but not let go of selling drugs. The money I was making was coming in so frequently, I didn't have to do pretty much anything, and I liked it that way. There were slow times where a few setbacks occurred, but that's why I always saved for those rainy days. Not wanting to lose the opportunity of trying something new, I went with my friend to sign up and receive my car dealer's license. Whenever I was free, I would ride with him to learn the ins & outs of the business. Starting to see how I could invest my money and make more by flipping cars, I started to purchase a few of my own vehicles. All the vehicles needed were a little fixing up and a method of marketing. I purchased four vehicles to advertise during income tax season. Nevertheless, I was arrested, thus putting a dent in my plans before I even had the opportunity to sell any one of them.

Straddling the fence will never pan out the way you think it may. When you're involved in any wrongdoings, it outweighs the good and will eventually catch up to you in some sort of way. See, I was arrested and accused once again of a crime that I did not commit, and with my previous record, it would be hard to exclude me from being a possible suspect. I wasn't innocent from breaking the law by far, it's just I hadn't been caught for some of the things that I had done. Faced with all types of challenges, now my life was getting ready to be challenged like never before. By me always wanting to remain comfortable, I wasn't allowing myself to grow. In life, you are always going to be faced with some type of challenge, but in order to move forward, you'll need to face them head on and not turn away from them. Being comfortable feels good at the time, but actually it hinders you from reaching your full potential. A lot of times this occurs because one is afraid to fail. However, failure is a part of the process, because how can you learn anything if you don't make mistakes?

Every great person has failed within their lives, but that doesn't make them a failure. They used their malfunction to get stronger. That's why their able to talk about how they succeeded in life, due to them embracing those challenges and fears. So if you're one to keep running from challenges you've faced in life, understand that you're only running from forward progress.

11

FEAR OF THE INEVITABLE

"You may not control all the events that happen
to you, but you can decide not to be reduced by them."
-Maya Angelou

On the evening of January 6, 2011, I was arrested and couldn't believe that I was in handcuffs once again. Although I tried doing well, trouble still seemed to come my way. With me straddling the fence, it was inevitable for something like this to take place in my life. Not expecting it to be of this magnitude, but the reality was it happened. The night that I was arrested, someone was shot in the area I was near, and according to some police officers, they had witnessed me commit the shooting. After hearing this, I just knew it was all a dream, well a nightmare actually. Where the incident took place, I never stepped foot on the premises, so anyone seeing me commit the shooting was impossible. Having gone through this process on different occasions, I wasn't expecting a bail by any means. My prior history with the judicial system had hindered me from any such relief. Now all I could rely on was hiring an attorney to prove my innocence.

Having no bail meant nothing but a trip back to the city jail. Knowing the conditions I was getting ready to be under, only added more stress to my situation. When I was arrested, a friend of mine was also with me, so we were pretty much together throughout the entire process. Given that it had been a few years since either one of us had been at the detention center, we were in for a rude awakening of what we were getting ready to be faced with. Over time things had changed, so the environment had gotten worse than before. The primary issue was gang activity. I was already expecting to be on lockdown for the majority of the time, but the way they were running things now, it was as if this was the world's most dangerous detention center. Once you were transported to the intake tier, you would then be transferred to certain sections according to the nature of your charge. This placed me in the category of a violent criminal and I was sent to a section which was considered maximum security. Not fully aware of my fear of the unavoidable, having the fortitude to get through was what helped.

Once we left the intake tier, my friend and I were transferred to J-section. We only slept 10 cells away from each other, but with this section being maximum security, we still didn't see one another. The correctional officer, or C.O., would only let two cells out at a time, and then would lock us in the dayroom. The only thing in the dayroom were two phones and if you didn't have anyone to call, you would just be locked inside a bigger cell. There was a specific time to shower, and that was on the 11PM-7AM shift. Again, it was two cells at a time, and you didn't know when they were going to get to your cell. Thus, if you were sleep and missed your door, you would have to wait until the next shower day. We were only able to shower every four days. There were four tiers on each section, and only one tier was getting a shower per day. Whenever we were transported throughout the jail, we were escorted in handcuffs. This singled us out from all the other sections that weren't considered maximum. My first 120 days were under these conditions but eventually they gave us a little more breathing room.

Upon headquarters receiving knowledge of how things were being ran in the detention center, the Warden was forced to give us more time out of our cells. By the jail being so affected with gang activity, they placed us on modified recreation, whereas, one tier would come out for 90 minutes at a time. In the 90 minute time span, we were able to shower and use the phone. In addition, my friend and I were able to come in contact with one another by us being on the same tier. Eventually, we moved into a cell together.

Faced with being around all those gang members, there was no telling what tomorrow would bring. At least 40% of the section was a part of one gang, so it was a battle each and every day. With a lot of the guys being younger, the fact that I hadn't been at the city jail in some years, I hardly knew anyone. This required my friend and I to just have each other's back. With the environment we were in, clearly only the strong survived. A lot of the gang members did things, such as bullying and terrorizing other inmates, only because there were a lot of them. Understanding that any given moment could be a call for war, getting a jail house knife was a must.

Being incarcerated, you had to adapt to your environment, and having a creative mind came with survival. With limited movement, it was hard to find anything to make a weapon out of. After getting to know a few of the guys on the tier and not being a gang member, we became cool and were lent a knife until we were able to get our own. Now I'm carrying it on my person every day, and I most certainly had the intent to use it in order to protect myself. Seeing all that was taking place before my eyes, it was better to be with a weapon, than without it. While my friend and I took turns taking showers, whoever was out of the shower would hold the knife and watch the other's back. What made matters worse; some of the correctional officers were on the same side the gang was on. Therefore, you had to be on point at all times. Ultimately, my friend and I were split up. Since he was a parole violator, he was sent to the Jessup Region where the violators were housed. As I continued on my journey, I only saw my friend on the days we had to appear in court.

Due to the process of constant postponements, I spent my first year on J-section. Since I was in the jail for some time now, I began to be well known by the staff, which gave me the opportunity to move to F-section. This section was a little better, but the gangs were all over the jail. I'd always considered myself to hold my own, so I didn't even worry about them too much. Although I had been in a few verbal altercations, they never got physical and I was known for being one who would not back down. The best thing about F-section was that it was an air-conditioned tier. That was because the tier was once a medical unit. So not being hot was definitely a blessing, but as soon as the summer hit, I gave that privileged up for what I believed was only right.

The city jail was full of excessive violence. Every time someone would get stabbed or beat up, they would lock us down and take our visits and commissary. After going through this over and over again my first year on J-section, to move to another section and get the same treatment was ridiculous to me. Besides, the guards would allow a lot of the incidents to take place. In addition, with the gang members having all the jobs on the tier, they would remain out of their cells after committing the violence, while the rest of us were still behind the grill trying to get a shower. This was frustrating, so all I wanted was to get out of this predicament. Over time, I asked for a job, which would allow me to stretch my legs a little. Receiving no results and constantly being on lock down, caused me to force their hand to place me in either solitary confinement or in a much better section.

One day after I showered, I decided that once I was done, I wasn't locking back in. With my bag already packed, as soon as I was done with my shower, I told the officer to call her supervisor because I wasn't going back into my cell. She locked me in the dayroom and I waited until the Sgt. and Lieutenant came. After telling them that I was tired of losing my privileges like visits and commissary and requesting to move to the dorms, they insisted on trying to get me to go back into my cell, and told me that they would move me very soon. They asked me was I willing to go on lock up for refusing housing and I articulated that I was already on lock up anyway. Once they came to the conclusion that I wasn't trying to hear what they had to say, I was then handcuffed and escorted to lock up.

Besides the fact of not having air conditioning, and me being in the cell alone, lock up was no different from F-section. Since the ticket that was written up on me was considered weak, I was offered another opportunity to go to another section similar to the two I had already been on. I refused the offer, because it was just going to place me back in the same tight spot. Determined to be housed in the dormitories, I stayed on solitary confinement for approximately a month. I then was told that I would be moving to P-section, which was one of the dormitories in the detention center. I knew a few guys that were housed in this section because they were workers throughout the jail so within the same week of my arrival, I was given a job.

Staying in the dorms was much better than the cells. I was able to take a shower at any time and we also had a TV. It had been 18 months since I had seen any television, so it was pleasing to watch. Plus, with the constant postponements every time I went to court, it allowed me not to stress as much. My job allowed me to come in contact with more staff by me being in the hallways a lot. Eventually,

I was given the best job I could have in the jail thanks to a buddy I was working with. There was a Lieutenant that he grew up with who worked at the jail. She liked the way I carried myself plus the fact that I wasn't gang affiliated helped. Having the privilege to move around anywhere throughout the jail on my own, I became very well-known with the staff as a result of my demeanor. But with my criminal addiction, the freedom I was given only allowed me to get involved with all the illegal activity that was going on in the city jail.

Baltimore City Detention Center was well known for criminal activity. The correctional officers were bringing in everything from tobacco, drugs, liquor, knives, money, cell phones, food and even having relationships with inmates. The majority of these transactions were taking place with the gang members. However, there were a chosen few that were not gang affiliated who also received the same benefits. Being well-known and a stand-up individual, I was for sure reaping some of the benefits. Fighting the attempted murder charge was very stressful, so as long as it was weed in the jail, I remained high. Having a cell phone was a must as well. It was something in high demand for those making money selling tobacco or any other drugs. And being able to have direct contact with those on the outside was a given advantage. This type of activity had been going on for years, and although it didn't cease completely, a big crack down took place.

In 2013, there was a huge federal indictment involving several correctional officers and the Black Guerrilla Family (BGF) gang members. According to the indictment, one of the C.O.'s had a baby by one of the gang members, and a few others were pregnant by him. A couple of guys indicted weren't even located at the city jail anymore but they were still charged with racketeering & wiretap charges. Seeing this whole ordeal unfold was a true eye opener, but it didn't stop me from continuing what I was doing. Since the gang members were the main target, I wasn't too concerned about getting caught up. Sick and tired of being locked up period, my only hope was that my case be dismissed or for me to start trial at my upcoming court date. After having 12 postponements, and sitting over in the city jail for almost three years, my case was finally set to go to trial. I was happy to finally start trial but I was also nervous and fearful of what the outcome could possibly be.

On May 13, 2013, I began the process of picking the jury. With me having a co-defendant, the selection of people to choose from were much larger than being on trial alone. Once concluding with picking the jury, I felt good with those that were selected. Knowing that I didn't commit the shooting, and the victim didn't identify me as the shooter, I was confident with going to trial. Even though I had the police saying they witnessed me commit the shooting, the evidence wasn't adding up with their statements. Throughout the trial, the description of the shooter was a major factor because the shooter was supposed to have been wearing a mask. The officer's description of the shooter was a tall and slim person fitting my height and build, but the friend of the victim gave a description stating that the shooter was much shorter and had a heavy build. The primary officer of the case had even went to the extent of saying he saw me toss the alleged gun used in the shooting. With the testimonies being so inconsistent, finding me guilty seemed so farfetched. But, with police officers considered to be one of the most believable human beings on earth, the jury came back with a guilty verdict after deliberation on May 24, 2013.

After the reading of all the charges, hearing the word guilty only left me numb and in total disbelief. Everything that was presented to the jury could not be considered beyond a reasonable doubt. There were so many inconsistencies within the police officers testimonies, so I didn't know how they could believe anything that was brought before them. Troubled by what was next, I had to return back to the jail wondering how much time I was going to receive. See, some things in life you aren't able to prepare for. However, remaining strong is a must. Even though I was a little stressed, I had a **Never Give In, Never Give Up** attitude. I knew I was facing a life sentence, but no matter how much time I was given, I told myself I was going to give it back. Even with that being my standpoint, I still was frightened of what was bound to happen. I knew that my life was going to be different, and it would affect my family as well.

Whenever you're faced with situations out of your control, do your best to stay positive. Understand it's a message in every lesson. You may not understand it at the time, but don't be held back by your circumstances. Allow it to make you stronger and be an inspiration for the individuals who are in a more tragic state of affairs than you are. Face those fears, because what's meant to be - shall be; only God knows what's best for you.

12

WAKE UP CALL

"When I was a child, I spoke as a child,
I understood as a child, I thought as a child, but
when I became a man, I put away childish things."
-1 Corinthians 13:11

Following my guilty verdict, my attorney filed a motion for a new trial, which had to be filed within ten days after the verdict. The motion was based upon the inconsistencies of the officers testimony and insufficient evidence. Shortly after my trial was over, I became aware of a surveillance video pertaining to the case. This evidence would have been a major factor in my trial, because of the discrepancy with the identification of the shooter. While I had asked my attorney about the surveillance footage when I first received my motion of discovery, he indicated that there wasn't any. Therefore, I left it alone, believing him I thought nothing else of it. Confronting him again after trial, he still denied the fact of having such evidence. I knew my co-defendant's lawyer had a copy of the video, so I asked my attorney to subpoena him to my motion for a new trial hearing to verify the video he had in his possession. My attorney then told me to call him back in a few days, so he could speak with the other attorney. Once I called him back, he mentioned that he reviewed the video, but there wasn't anything helpful to the case. With that sounding hard to believe, I asked him to bring the video to the city jail so I could review it myself, and he told me that he couldn't bring his equipment in the jail. I knew that was a lie. Eventually, I had a friend go review it at his office and she confirmed what I already knew, that I wasn't on the video.

On the block where the shooting had occurred, there was a liquor store on the corner with a camera positioned to capture footage on the front of the store. The State's theory was that I had walked past the liquor store, committed the shooting, and then ran back towards the direction that I came from. While the shooting hadn't taken place on camera, I certainly should've been in the view of the camera at least on 2 different occasions, walking by and running back pass the camera. Since I wasn't, the video wasn't used by the State's attorney. As to why my lawyer didn't use it, I didn't have a clue. With the help from a buddy of mine, I then filed a supplemental petition for the motion for new trial pertaining to the surveillance video, along with an attorney grievance on my lawyer. Once my attorney received the complaint against him, he then filed a motion to withdraw his appearance on my case. At the time, my motion for new trial/sentencing hearing was already scheduled for August 28, 2013. But with our difference of opinion taking place, when I appeared at the hearing, the judge gave me the opportunity to postpone the hearing in order to hire another attorney.

Prior to my arrest, I still was on probation from the sentence I had of six years. Only having four months left on probation when I was arrested for the current charges, I had violated my probation. When the violation was put forward, I was given a court date, which continued to be postponed until after the final outcome of the current charges. Following my trial date, my hearing for my violation was set for September 5, 2013, and at this court hearing I had a big decision to make. Even though I had already been found guilty of the charges brought against me, I had the option to either go forth with my probation hearing, or postpone it until after my motion for new trial/sentencing hearing. I was facing seven years for my violation case and life for the attempted murder charge. My thoughts were, if my motion for new trial was to be denied, that seven years wouldn't mean anything compared to the amount of time I would receive. I also thought that my chances of getting the entire seven years were very slim, due to my good behavior while I was on probation. Either way, I had almost three years in, which was about half of the seven, so I was almost finished doing that sentence. Still undecided, once I got into the courtroom, as well as tired of sitting over at the city jail, I decided to proceed with my hearing. After trying to explain to the judge that I was innocent of my conviction, she listened only to express that I was considered to be a menace to society and sentenced me to the entire seven years.

Receiving the probation time had placed me on the list to be sent to prison. I had to be classified before I was transferred to the prison institution. Even with having close to half of the seven years in, my points would go up due to my pending case. This caused my security level to be medium. Once I was classified, I then knew I would be leaving Baltimore City jail any day. Therefore, on September 23, 2013, I packed up and was sent to Roxbury Correctional Institute in Hagerstown, MD.

On the ride to Hagerstown, I started to have a different outlook on life. I knew things were getting ready to change, and the fact of the matter was, I didn't know how. I currently had seven years upon my arrival, however, I didn't know how things were going to turn out for me once I went back for my upcoming sentencing. One thing for sure, I had no control over what the judge was going to do, but as for me, changing for the better was a must. In spite of my circumstances, I had to remain strong and work on self, something I've never done before. My court date was set for December 12, 2013, but it had gotten postponed because my new attorney was not prepared or available for that date. In the midst of me still not knowing my fate, altering my thinking was something I did know.

Growing up, my family was always involved in church. Although I didn't want to go and was forced to go, deep down inside, it was embedded in me to serve God. Like I mentioned back in Chapter 2, Proverbs 22:6 states: "Train up a child in the way he should go, and when he is old, he will not depart from it." I am a true example of that passage and by me reaching that point of my life where I was starting to see things clearer than before, I turned back to what was considered to be my roots. In prison, you have different religious services that you're able to attend. So, after requesting to be placed on the non-denomination service list, my request was granted. I started attending service every Sunday. I've always believed in God, but I never accepted Him in my life to direct my path. I thought I could do it my way, but I had finally realized that my way wasn't working. Being fully aware of this, and due to me truly having the desire to change, on December 31, 2013, I accepted Jesus Christ as my Lord and Savior.

Accepting Christ in my life has given me a peace within that I've never experience before. Even with all that I was up against, I was still able to be positive about my situation. This caused me to not just work on my spiritual self, but on my intellect as well. Gaining wisdom and receiving as much knowledge as I could was my focus at this point. When I first arrived at Roxbury, I signed up for any program I thought was going to help with my transformation in life. With recommendations from a few of the guys I was around, I joined several different programs. This removed me out of my comfort zone, because interacting with a group of men I didn't even know, had never been my thing. However, it helped me grow and be the man that I am today.

With my court date coming soon, spending my time in the law library was also very important. I wanted to be prepared for my motion for a new trial hearing. While noticing an error within the verdict given for one of the charges, I brought it to my attorney's attention, and she prepared to address it at the hearing. After receiving a guilty verdict almost a year ago, April 28, 2014 was my day in court to see what was next for me. The hearing began with my attorney addressing the inconsistent verdict for the conspiracy charges, which by law you couldn't find one person guilty of the charge, and the other not guilty after appearing in a joint trial. Having the case law to back it up, the motion to vacate the conspiracy verdict was heard and then granted. We then moved on to the surveillance video argument. The argument was pertaining to me not being in the video, and the fact that my trial attorney never showed me the footage. My lawyer explained the inconsistency in the officer's testimony, and had the surveillance video been played during the trial, the outcome of trial may have been different. The State rebuttal was that it wasn't legible, and my supplemental petition wasn't done in a timely manner. With the judge hearing both sides, she decided to hold the decision sub curia, letting me know I would receive the decision in the mail. Feeling good with how the hearing turned out, I went back to Roxbury with high hopes of being granted a new trial. Unfortunately, that wasn't the case. On July 31, 2014, my motion was denied and my sentencing date was set for December 1, 2014.

When I received the judge's decision, I stared at the word DENIAL for about 10 minutes, not believing what I saw. All I could think of was how much time was I going to receive. Even though I was disappointed, I wasn't going to let that deter my spirit. In the past I would have smoked marijuana and drank alcohol to cope with the circumstances. However, having a different outlook on life, I now decided to remain sober and use prayer as my coping mechanism. I had faith in God, and I knew whatever was to come my way, He was going to help me get through it. My main goal at the time was to work on self, because I genuinely wanted to find myself and be better than I had ever been before. I continued to tell myself that I wasn't going to spend the rest of my life behind bars or do whatever time I was given. Therefore, change had to start now, so that's why I attended different self-help groups and thought about my career in the future. While learning something from all of the programs I attended, two of them were of true benefit for me, Men 4 Life and a Commercial Driver's License (CDL) class. Men 4 Life was a program where a group of men of different religions and perceptions on life came together as one big think tank. We had homework assignments, which required 3-5 page essays, and spoke on several different subjects dealing with societal issues and performance on public speaking. Out of the three, public speaking was for sure my weakest component, however this program gave me some confidence to strengthen my effort. With my writings, I had become aware of the gift I had all along. As for the CDL program, I was always interested in the trucking industry, so I wanted to take advantage of having the opportunity to take the course and learn all that I could. Changing my way of thinking had allowed me to have the courage to try something different, and be more efficient in doing so.

Everyone is given a wake-up call. Some are from learning from others experiences, while others are from experiences of your own. Only you can be tired of making the same mistakes, and decide to change your way of thinking. When a child is born, they're ignorant to a lot of things until they receive the proper guidance. Once that child has reached the level to comprehend what has been taught, applying that information to their way of living comes next. When you're an adult, thinking and acting as a child should cease to exist.

Although I was an adult in age, I continued to act, speak and think childishly. With me being ignorant to my childish affairs, it only held me back from receiving what God has in store for me. While as long as you have breath in your body, it's never too late. Taking heed to

68

your wake-up call will position you to be in the very place God intends for you to be.

13

GOD'S TIMING

*"In life, what sometimes appears to be the
end is really a beginning."*
-Unknown

December 1, 2014, was not only my sentencing date, but my 33rd birthday as well. I wasn't sure if the judge paid any attention to this date being my birthday or not, but I was about to receive one heck of a present. Knowing that I had the possibility of receiving a life sentence, all I could do was pray and let God handle the rest. I knew this date wasn't set by accident; it was certainly a part of God's plan. What made this day more noteworthy was that the young lady I was in love with back in high school was standing right before my eyes in the midst of all my family and friends supporting me on this day. We had always stayed in contact with one another, but hadn't seen each other in approximately 10 years. Therefore, it was shocking for me to see her there, and regardless of the time I was facing, she remained on my mind.

Before I came up into the courtroom, my lawyer had come and seen me in the bull pen. Her thoughts were that I was going to receive a sentence of life plus 20 years for the charges I was convicted of, along with my criminal background. She mentioned that she was going to ask the judge for a life sentence, all suspended but 20 years. I wasn't feeling her request at all, so I just went back to sit down. I told the Lord that His will shall be done. I will say I was a little nervous, but I honestly didn't care what I was sentenced to, because I wasn't expecting to do the entire time I was given anyhow. I just looked at it as a minor set-back, for a major come-back. For that reason, I was a firm believer that justice was going to be served in God's time, and not mine.

Sitting in the courtroom listening to the State's Attorney speak about the type of person she thought I was, was relatively interesting. Although I did have a lengthy record, I most definitely wasn't a danger to society. Throughout my past, I'd made a lot of poor decisions at times, and was falsely accused on others, including my current situation. Deep down inside, I felt like she knew I didn't commit this crime, nevertheless it was her job to try and send me to prison. While she was asking the judge to sentence me to life in prison, what God had in store for me was already in the making. There were a lot of people there on my behalf at the hearing, but my mother, eldest brother, and uncle were chosen to speak as my character witnesses. When it was my attorney's time to speak on my behalf to ask for her sentence recommendation, the judge instantly started speaking to me, letting me know I had the right to speak and not give my lawyer the chance to even ask for the sentence she had mentioned to me. This day was truly all about me, and having the opportunity to speak on behalf of myself, I took advantage of that very moment. I've always professed my innocence, and at the time of this sentencing, I was on the verge of graduating the CDL class; as well as enrolled in a few other programs. Receiving a life sentence would have placed me in a maximum security prison, and made me ineligible for any rehabilitative programs. So, after I asked the judge for a ray of hope and the opportunity to complete the courses I was currently involved in, she considered my request, and sentenced me to 25 years, with the possibility of parole. The judge had also requested for my attorney to file a Motion for Modification of Sentence, which she would hold sub curia until a later date, and ordered for me to remain at R.C.I.

Once I arrived back at Roxbury, I instantly called my mom. After hearing what the judge said to me at my hearing, she told me that I was going to be fine. My next phone call was immediately to my younger cousin, so I could call my high school sweetheart on the 3-way. She answered right away, and the both of us were just as excited to hear from the other. Our conversation was based upon us not seeing each other in so long. Seeing one another in person had only let the both of us know we were still very much in love. Not knowing how things were going to turn out after receiving a 25 year sentence, she claimed her position as my lady and told me that she wasn't going anywhere. This couldn't have happened at a better time. Since my mentality had changed, God had blessed me with a beautiful, strong, encouraging woman. After all I'd been through, I was well equipped with what I needed to know on how to appreciate a woman the way I should. That's why God waited for the right time to place her back into my life.

A few weeks later, my attorney sent me a letter letting me know she had filed a Notice of Appeal, and the Motion for Modification/Sentencing Reduction to be held sub curia. Enclosed with the letter was a copy of what she had submitted. Given that this was the end of her representation pertaining to my case, she informed me to stay out of trouble and to request for my modification to be heard in about three years. I was already on the right track, so staying out of trouble was not a problem. However, on January 12, 2015, the judge denied my modification, and didn't hold it sub curia like she suggested at my hearing. I was truly confused, because after everything she had said at my sentencing hearing, it didn't make sense for her to deny the motion. What's more upsetting is that I withdrew my appeal the same day the denial was ordered, due to a lack of knowledge. I really was banking on my sentence getting reduced as long as I had stayed focused and did what I was supposed to do. By me not receiving the maximum sentence, I thought if I was to win my appeal and lose trial again, I could receive the max, which played a major part in my decision. I didn't have but so much time to make up my mind, and after gaining the knowledge I needed at the time, I realized it was pretty much a bad move on my behalf. This caused a big headache, and some doubt, but I remained strong knowing that this wasn't the end, because I was going to continue to fight.

Still believing that this was a misunderstanding, I wrote the judge explaining my confusion and not having the opportunity to do anything she had asked of me. My letter was written for the motion to be held sub curia, and not heard at that time. After not receiving a response within the next 10 months, I decided to write her again hoping to at least hear back from her. While I was patiently waiting, I continued to study my case and started working on my post-conviction petition. I couldn't let that situation keep me stagnated, I wasn't cool with just being in prison. With me more conscious and aware of the value of freedom, I was determined to get from behind these walls. I still hadn't heard anything from the judge, so my next step was to hire an attorney to see if I could get some results. After speaking with a lawyer a friend of mine recommended, she was appalled by the situation, and was willing to try and help me. I sent her everything that I filed to the courts, along with the transcript from my sentencing hearing, where the judge's direct order was given. On August 16, 2016, my attorney filed a Motion to Correct Mistake in Ruling on Motion for Modification of Sentence, which was denied on August 25, 2016. With my attorney and I still confused, she decided to continue to assist me with no additional charge, while I kept working on my post-conviction.

Even with all of this going on, I still continued to attend different programs, working on self and trying to help others. With my experience and connection with guys younger than me, I decided to join a program called Youth Challenge. Youth Challenge was a course designed for young men, ages 25 and under, dealing with goal setting, communication skills, accountability and much more. Having a lot to offer, I became a facilitator to give the guys another outlook on life. Understanding that it wasn't going to be an easy task, I felt if I could reach just one individual, I'd succeeded within my mission. This was absolutely a big step for me, because I've always been a negative example to those younger than me. While all of the programs issued a certificate of completion, only Youth Challenge and the Men 4 Life program allowed us to invite two guests listed on our visiting list to attend graduation. Both groups worked on public speaking, and although that wasn't my strong point, I was chosen to speak at the Men 4 Life graduation and host the Youth Challenge graduation. Having my lady and mother see and hear me speak from behind the podium was a wonderful feeling. The smiles on their faces allowed me to see how proud I had made them both. I knew that this was just the beginning of me being great, so I continued to participate in more programs, while still working on my case.

Innocent of the charges brought against me, I knew that I had several legitimate claims to address. I studied my case regularly, and with the help from a buddy of mine who was considered a jail house lawyer, we were making progress with the petition. The lawyer was still working on the modification motion, and on January 4, 2017, she filed a Motion to Hold a Timely Filed Motion for Modification of Sentence sub curia. The judge had already denied this matter on two different occasions, so I wasn't expecting anything different this time around. I actually was ready to file my post-conviction petition, but a friend of my uncle, who worked in the public defender's office at the time, was reviewing the claims within my petition. While waiting on feedback from her, I had my lady call the lawyer to see if any ruling on the motion had been made. Once I spoke back with my lady, she informed me that the lawyer told her that the motion was once again denied, but then told me within her next breath, that the primary officer on my case, Detective Daniel Hersl, had been arrested. Throughout the years, I told her this officer was crooked, and even had her look him up on several different occasions to see if something like this had occurred. So when the news broke, I wasn't surprised at all. On March 1, 2017, seven Baltimore City Police Department Officers were arrested for racketeering conspiracy, and racketeering offenses; including robbery, extortion, and overtime fraud. Det. Hersl was the most important witness in my case, and with this indictment taking place, his credibility holds no value. Realizing that my case was truly affected by the arrest of this officer, I then went forward with filing my post-conviction petition on April 6, 2017.

The indictment of these officers was the face of the news, and several cases were being dropped because of their corrupt activity. The State's Attorney's office was focusing on cases from 2015 up until the officer's arrest. However, the public defender's office argument was that these officers didn't just become crooked in 2015; this was ongoing behavior, so currently a number of cases are under review. With me being able to amend my petition, I filed my original petition in order to start the process and receive a court date. Following the filing of my petition, my buddy helped me put a supplemental petition together addressing Det. Hersl's corrupt activity, which didn't allow me to have a fair trial. The State responded to my initial petition and the judge set a court date for November 6, 2017. After receiving the court date, I was assigned an attorney from the Post-Conviction Defenders Division. Furthermore, Det. Daniel Hersl along with two other officers from the initial indictment was re-indicted for additional robbery charges on July 6, 2017. With my situation getting better day-by-day, I'm patiently waiting for my day in court.

Before I even filed my post-conviction petition, my buddy explained the procedure and the steps it would take once the ball got rolling. He also told me that he hoped I would be appointed a particular attorney in the Post-Conviction Defenders Division. He spoke highly of this guy, and explained his hunger as an attorney. While I wasn't too confident in using a public defender, I still was seeking private counsel. Not long after I had received my court date, I received a letter from my appointed representation, which happened to be the same guy my buddy spoke of. Naive to the sign, I still continued to reach out for private counsel. The attorney I was seeking had visited me and after we discussed my case, he stated he couldn't represent the case for less than $25,000. While feeling my freedom was worth more than that, I still was worried about trying to come up with that amount of money. But once I prayed on it, and asked God to speak to me, He made things clear. I decided to just go along with the public defender. It wasn't a coincidence that I received the exact same attorney on my case that my buddy mentioned, and I was about to miss the very blessing that God had presented right before my eyes. So, after making the decision to stick with the appointed attorney, I wrote him, letting him know I was looking forward to meeting him and discussing my case.

On September 12, 2017, the attorney came to see me and I expected the visit to be more than it was, because of all that was going on with my case. Once I sat down with him, I learned that he hadn't started to review my case. He asked me was I okay with him requesting a postponement, because he wanted to be fully prepared to argue my claims. Not wanting him to be fully prepared would've been foolish of me, so I explained, if that was needed, of course I was okay with him postponing the case. I also wanted to know could he request for a deal that would get me out of prison. I explained that I was willing to take a deal right now, because I wanted to get home to my family, but if I had to wait it out, I wasn't going to take any deal. Since I knew my case, and the fact that this officer was in jail, the State's Attorney should be glad I wanted to consider taking a deal. As I continued to stress my need for him to seek a deal, he said he would speak with the State's Attorney, but first wanted me to send him a copy of my accomplishments since I'd been incarcerated.

Before our departure, he asked me about a date of September 13, 2016 dealing with the Court of Special Appeals that was located on my court docket entry. I told him that I had no idea, because I hadn't filed anything with them. He left letting me know he'd be in touch. The following week I received a letter from him explaining the date of September 13, 2016, which was the mandate set from my appeal that I withdrew. According to Maryland Rule 4-331(c) based on newly discovered evidence, you have a year from the date of the appellate mandate to file a motion under this rule. So that meant I only had until September 13, 2017 to file it, which was the very next day after he came and saw me. In his letter he informed me that once he got back to the office, he got it done right away and filed it on time, arguing that the DNA testing was inaccurate and the officer's indictment produced an unfair trial. Not knowing how things are going to turn out, and which court date will come first, I'm just being patient, preparing for my next chapter in life.

Going into my sentencing hearing seemed as if it was the end of my life, but actually it was a new beginning. While most expected for me to receive life in prison, I was sentenced to 25 years instead. Even after getting this large amount of time at the age of 33, God also blessed me with a beautiful, strong woman to help me get through the most difficult time of my life. I had finally decided to be a better man, which allowed me to position myself to receive what God intended for me all along. Although He was blessing me, I still had to experience a few essential interruptions. This showed me how testing only makes you stronger, and there is a season for everything. It has been said by Mr. Frederick Douglass, "Without any struggle, there couldn't be any progress", and this struggle has given me a testimony to share God's greatness with others.

See, all the events that has taken place had to happen on God's time, because if it was up to me, I wouldn't have gone through any of this. However, this was my season to tell my story, and God knew that it couldn't have been at a better time.

14

THE MESSAGE

"Though no one can go back and make a brand new start,
anyone can start from now and make a brand new ending."
-Carl Bard

Wherever you are in life, it cost you something to get there. Most of us would consider doing things a lot differently if we had the opportunity to do it all over again. Yet, you must realize that your past experiences have shaped who you are today. Making sure your ending is a complete turnaround from your beginning is what you should be aiming for in your life. See, that's where I am today. I can't erase my past, I just have to use my present to work on my future. Years ago, I would have never thought of writing a book, but when you make the necessary changes you know you should make for personal growth, you'll be surprised at what you're capable of doing. Throughout my life, I've been trying to fulfill a void that I'd always held within. After coming around and seeing life much clearer, I started to understand that life was much more than what I was making it out to be.

The most important thing I've learned about myself is that I needed spiritual nutrition in my life. Being fully aware that there is a true Creator of all things, it had to be something greater within me than what I was demonstrating. Missing that spiritual connection with God was only hindering me from finding my purpose for living. Since I was born a child of God, the spiritual connection has always been there. I was just too busy avoiding His warning signals, so I continued to travel down the wrong path. The good thing is, He never gave up on me, and He just used my failure and turned it into a success story. With all the mistakes I've made, they have only allowed me to gain the wisdom that I currently possess. Now I realize that sharing what God has blessed me with is a part of my purpose.

I believe that no one goes through life without searching for something. Whether its love, peace, acceptance, a vision, and their purpose for being here on earth and more, we all are looking to find **that missing piece**. My experience in prison has caused me to see this at face value. With having the opportunity to witness guys join one religious group to the next, as well as in and out of gangs, only leads me to believe they're trying to find something that's missing. The same is within our society, when you have individuals jumping from one relationship to another, and continually changing their careers. This is because it's natural for us to want more than what we have, which leaves us undecided or confused on what we really want.

There are a lot of things that can influence your search in life, so you must find out who you are as an individual and be careful who you are giving your time to. You must eliminate negative thinking, as well as negative company. That energy will affect how you move in life. As you continue to grow in life, a lot of things are going to change, including your associates. Everyone doesn't want you to move forward in life, but the question is: What do you want? Make sure you are careful where you stop to inquire for directions along the road of life.

No matter what your current situation may be, it's never too late to get your dreams off the ground, you just have to believe in yourself. How things started out for you, doesn't have to remain that way. You must first start with self, and you'll begin to learn what you're searching for. What's important is to not allow your situation to go from bad to worse, which means you must change your mentality. To relocate with the same intentions, only shows that the lessons you've experienced hasn't taught you anything. Don't devote yourself to anything that's continuously causing you to fail. We all are faced with adversity, but you shouldn't choose your adverse circumstances willingly.

As long as you're reluctant to change, you're just wasting your opportunities here on earth, and delaying the process for you to become great. Therefore, accept the challenges that you're up against, because running from them, you're just agreeing to remain weak and stagnated. It's a fact that you can't control everything that comes your way, and it may cause fear, nevertheless you must face those fears with confidence and courage to receive growing success. In order to be conscious of your wake-up calls, you have to take heed to proper guidance and pay attention to your mistakes as well as the mistakes of others. At the end of the day, it'll be God's timing on whatever is meant for you. Don't fail to position yourself so you can receive the message that He has specifically for you.

My life has been a complete turnaround, beginning with the way I think. Up until I gained my relationship with God, I didn't have a clue as to what my purpose in life was. While I'm still not completely sure of it, I do know that doing my best to be better than I was yesterday is why I'm here. I've made a lot of poor choices in my past, and that's part of the reason why I'm in prison right now. Although I'm innocent of the charges I've been convicted of, one will always answer for the wrong that they have done one way or another - just like the cop in my case.

You may not understand why things happen the way they do, but that's only for God to know. He has a plan and a purpose for each one of our lives, and the purpose for my incarceration was to tell you that good can come from adversity. However, you must gain that closeness with God, because that's where true peace comes from. So, as we all are here trying to find what's truly missing, bear in mind that there's a space within us that only God can fulfill.

"Character cannot be developed in ease in quiet. Only through experience of trial and suffering can the soul be strengthened, ambition inspired, and success achieved."

~Hellen Keller

Volume 1, Issue 1   Summer 2017

BEHIND THE WALL MENTORS
NEWSLETTER
OPEN LETTERS TO THE YOUTH OF AMERICA

FROM: Author Shawn Gardner & Behind The Wall Mentors

SUBJECT: Words of Realness

Salutations, My Future Young Leaders Of The World

First and foremost, I pray that all is well as you read this inscribe. My name is Shawn Gardner, I was born in Baltimore City. I'm the founder of Behind the Wall Mentors. I'm also a published author of two books. One is an urban novel "A Hustlaz Dreams & Nightmares", and the other one is a children's book titled, "The Morals & Principle Pals-In the Track Meet". I started Behind the Wall Mentors so I could reach the youth of America, so that you could strive to make positive decisions in life, and become role models for the next generation. That way we break the cycle of madness and chaos in our communities. I want to afford you all the opportunity that I didn't receive when I was young. I'm a firm believer that a wise man or woman can learn from the bad decisions they make. But you're considered a genius if you can learn from others bad decisions.

If you all haven't heard it yet, I want you to hear it from me first; the street life that everybody is glorifying is a dead end street! Just like the board game Monopoly, you go straight to jail, don't past go, and don't collect your $200.00.

The only thing about this game is that it's real life and sometimes you don't get out. And you definitely can't wait three turns or role doubles. And it's not like Grand Theft Auto when you can just turn the game off. They don't call it the Trap for nothing. All that is really promised in the Trap is a two man little jail cell or a shiny casket. A friend of mine said it best when he told a young man we were mentoring, that one way or another the streets will leave you R.l.P., Resting In Prison or Resting In Peace. I'm not here to try to scare you; I just want you to know the reality of being about that Trap Life. The deck is stacked and the odds are always against you. The judicial system has laws in place where you will end up fighting for your life in prison, and, that's when everything comes full circle. You realize who your true family and friends are. Believe me the most hurtful feeling in the world is when one of your love ones or friends can tell you, on one hand, that they love you and then on the other hand, they leave you high and dry. Sadly, it is done without attempting to throw you a life preserver so you at least don't drown. I'm telling you it's another world behind these walls. So beware of the consequences of your acts of life, because if you come behind these walls, it will be you against the world. I've seen men lose their minds from being caged in for 23 hours a day. Even worst, I've seen correctional officers lose their minds from just watching convicts caged in for 23 hours a day. Now you see why I say, it's a whole different world behind these walls.

When it comes to the judicial system, I've seen it all and heard it all, on how Lady Justice's scales of justice isn't weighed right from the start if you don't have any money for an attorney. Now your life is in the hands of a Public Defender who is over worked, with little resources. Take it from me, I'm a perfect example. Yet, no matter what, I'll keep fighting my case. I've read guys trial transcripts and see how they paid their lawyers who then threw them to the wolves. So make sure you know your rights dealing with the law. I've seen prosecutors withheld impeachment evidence and other evidence, and even paid their witnesses to testify on their behalf. Now where is the justice in that? I want to save you and your families the headaches of having to experience this tragedy.

In closing, I hope that y'all are able to think before you act and try to stay surrounded by positive people. Also, never put yourself in a position that you have no control over, because you don't want to be the next

Freddie Gray or the millions of people locked up fighting for their lives. You Matter and that's the bottom line to this open letter.

Thank you for your time. I hope that y'all receive this inscribe in the spirit in which it was written. Namely total respect, honor, integrity and loyalty.

Stay peaceful!

TO THE YOUTH OF AMERICA

Greetings to the future,

My name is Marco Lomax and I'm currently incarcerated at Roxbury Correctional Institute in Hagerstown, Maryland. I'm here with a 25 years sentence, and I've currently been incarcerated for 6 years. I just would like to speak to you all on my experience and give you truth with this here life we're living. Growing up in the streets, being attracted to and apart of all the wrong things is what led me to prison today. Not taking education seriously or listening to my parent's advice was a major mistake. When you're young, you don't see what the adults in your life are trying to tell you, but hear me out, they are doing it for your own good. By them being here on earth years before you, they know the outcomes of all the decisions that you make. It's true that most have done it all or seen it all, so trying to prevent you from making the same mistakes seen or done is what there mainly trying to do and this is what I'm doing for you today through this open letter.

Life behind this wall is no joke, none what so ever. You have some that will never receive the opportunity to touch there love ones physically, get to see their kids grow; get visits or even have anyone to call. While living with a stranger whom you never met before, that can lose their mind at any given time, due to not being able to handle the pressure that's given behind these walls, on top of being rushed to eat some food that's not even cooked and can cause all types of illnesses such as diabetes and high blood pressure due to poor food selections. These are just a few things that occur on a daily basis, and I would like to say that it's not to scare you; however, I do want you to be afraid of coming to a place like this. This is no way to live, mainly because this isn't living it's just existing. You all have an opportunity in front of you to do whatever you would like to do, as long as you put your mind to it and never stop trying. The reason why I'm writing you today is because of something I live by, "NEVER GIVING IN & NEVER GIVING UP". And my duty today is to "NEVER GIVE IN, NOR UP ON THE YOUTH"!!

It's important to set goals, write them down and push hard to accomplish them. Remember education is the key, and keys open doors, so don't lock yourself out of life and from opportunities. Learn from your mistakes and most importantly learn from others mistakes, which is the wisest thing you can do. To continue to make the same wrong turn is foolish, and can lead to death quicker than expected. Why not make the right turn, and feel good about yourself for doing the best you can. Accountability and responsibility play a major part in our lives, you should always own up to the decisions and choices you've made, and always remember that no choice is also a choice you will have to live with. So not doing something can be detrimental to your life, especially if you know it's the right thing to do. Although the task may be hard, it must be done, and always remember that helping others out can be your tool to success, so try helping out those who don't know what you've learned. Striving for greatness and not settling is what I want from you all and know that it's more out of life than the streets. Stay in school and use the streets as your classroom to teach those the right way to turn. I would like to leave you with this quote, "Freedom is nothing but a chance to be better"; so stay free and go out and find who you have not yet become!! Thank you for listening to what I had to say, but take heed and apply yourself each and every day you wake up. I leave with respect, love and peace!!

FROM: MR. MARCO LOMAX A YOUTH CHALLENGE & BEHIND THE WALL MENTOR SUBJECT: TRUE WORDS OF REALNESS

Greetings, young men and women. My name is Terry Carter and I am writing you this letter with the intent of sharing a few words to illustrate the experiences that led to my current incarceration as well as encouragement for you to avoid the behavior and thinking that resulted in my present circumstances.

As a young man growing up in the D.C. metro area, I was exposed to and experienced firsthand what we called then, "Thug -Life." It was a way of viewing the outside world as an enemy in order for me to deal with the pain of poverty while also providing an excuse to take advantage of those with similar conditions just to fulfill my own selfish desires.

As an adolescent, I endured a variety of abuse from parental neglect to witnessing countless acts of violence that taught me to hate and be fearful of the outside world. I became angry and believed in my mind that conflict and confusion were the normal way of life.

Utilizing that thinking, my teenage years were spent committing numerous crimes stemming from the idea of myself being special and above the law. However, in reality I failed to realize that my thoughts and actions compromised my value as a human being and had the opposite effect. By choosing to harm instead of help, to take instead of give, I forfeited the right of my freedom and was sentenced to Life at the age of eighteen.

Too many times we allow ourselves to be influenced by the negative image of our communities. We choose to accept that these images are an accurate representation of reality, but in truth is misleading and destructive. Any idea or action that results in someone's suffering is simply not "right". And to believe otherwise is not only wrong-headed but wrong-hearted.

Although you may be suffering the realities of poverty as I have, you must not allow your outer conditions to define your inner self-image. Who you are is not the sum of what you possess, but what you produce. A person's ultimate value is in offering their talents to others rather than using them solely for themselves.

Think about it, which is more rewarding, being someone that your friends view as a good person and like to be around, or as someone to avoid and is disliked because of how they treat others. In this era of social media where a person's reputation is the most important factor in developing a following, what you are known for determines your popularity. Likewise, in life, your actions determine how you are perceived and what you become known for.

In conclusion, I would offer this final piece of advice. Enjoy your youth and don't rush to adulthood. Be very careful of the company you keep and the activities that you participate in. Remember, if what you're doing has to be hidden and kept secret then it's probably wrong.

Know that I believe in you and have faith that you will make the best of your life. Be great in your aspirations. I look forward to your success.

Sincerely,

Terry Carter-Behind the Wall Mentors

"Education is the most powerful weapon which you can use to change the world." Nelson Mandela

To those like me that could use a little advice,

It's crazy, we don't ask to be born, at least not to my knowledge, yet we encounter situations and circumstances way beyond our control. In my case to be here a black male in the 80's to what would be a single mother in D.C., says low success rate. It's as if my chance for survival or making it in any way was doomed from the start. You can check the statistics if you don't believe me.

Beyond the things I couldn't control here's what also happened: I was influenced by some of the wrong people. My mother, family, and Sunday school all told me what was right, but it was older cousins, friends at school and others who showed me what was cool. Even as an honor roll student, I was attracted to that "gangster" lifestyle, pimping and hustling. I mean they got the respect, women, and money. What else is there, right? So with the reinforcement of music and movies, I was feeding myself the wrong stuff. Not too far later drugs and alcohol came into the mix. Oh yea and sex.

These things can all be very confusing to a young man without the counsel of a much wiser man to guide him. Then there's the other things our community lacks, financial, education, emotional and psychological development, time management, and future planning. As my mother suffered financial setback, I was going through my teenage years and having self-esteem issues. We all know how school can be and the importance of being fly.

As a young man, I desired to be with those young ladies, but some of the things that attracted the ones that were willing to do some of the things I sought, I just didn't have. You couldn't tell me I was too young to be having sex or not mature enough to deal with my emotions or the young ladies that I may have been dealing with. I see it now after broken relationships, heartache, betrayal, S.T.D.'s, and a daughter. Then there's the image and money issues that even as I was beginning to recognize some things I haven't even skimmed the surface of. I think that there's something about being young that makes it extremely difficult to understand and practice patience. Not having the experience makes it even more difficult to have the foresight to prepare and plan for the future. Everything is now. Who cares or knows what it is to invest and for what? Well, everything is now, and if you aren't preparing and investing in yourself now, you'll look back wondering where the time went or upset that you hadn't taken advantage of some opportunities. One of the things I discovered is that everything I wanted to know, and I mean everything, could be found in a book. The most valuable resource available to me other than my own mind that I regret not using is the library. For whatever success I wanted could be learned, researched and developed with the aid of the books and resources there.

There are no women for me in prison and even though I have matured to value, and respect women, I have the understanding more so was to realize that I must become that which I want to attract. In other words if I want a good woman I have to become a good man. Oh, and the drug thing. Addiction and charges add up. From alcohol, I went to marijuana, from that to PCP; from that ecstasy, from that powder cocaine, and from that Percocet's. I've got a felony possession with the intent, which was my first charge that made it difficult for me to get employment. Along with that are a long line of possession, DUI, DWI, and the ghost of all the bad relationships, places I've been, things I've encountered and run-ins with the law. I hate being cuffed, I hate being placed in squad cars, I hate being processed, and I hate being pepper sprayed. I thought I was having fun getting high, but ain't nothing fun about recovering when your body crashes, a hangover, having your stomach pumped, or being in an accident and waking up in a hospital bed cuffed with citations. Rock star life style might not make it. I lived that stuff rappers talk about. The difference is they entertaining you all with stories. I am living the consequences and now I'm trying to give you a warning. You gonna do what you want though. I did.

S. Russell

An Open Letter

My name is Andre Young. I'm incarcerated doing 30 years, because of my destructive life style. I caused pain and hurt to my family as well as others. I've been locked up since I was 19 years old. I lived that life that rappers an TV are glorifying. I know firsthand it's almost impossible to win.

Now I choose to use my voice as a positive influence on the youth of today, tomorrow and so on because you are our future. That way you all can guild my future children. Being incarcerated for 13 years of my life has allowed me to introspectively look at my life and what led me here. In doing so, I take full responsibility for my actions because I know I made poor choices; Poor choices that have caused a snowball effect that led to my incarceration.

Here are some of the poor choices that I made which led me down the wrong path. I hope you can learn from my poor choices.

- Not listening to my parents. I remember how I would not listen to my parents who took care of me, but I would go out into the streets and listen to guys that didn't have my best interest at heart.
- Drinking and Drugging. I allowed this to cloud my judgment and to enhance my chances of making bad decisions. It ultimately had a negative impact on my health. My father died from corrosion of the liver at the age of 50, 18 months into my incarceration. His father died of the same thing around the same age due to their alcohol addiction. Why put yourself through that?
- Not valuing my free education. I was hooking school to hustle in the street, which was a bad choice. In life, you need math skills to count all that money you want. You need to know how to read and write. The further you take your education, the more opportunities and doors you can open. Hooking school sets the stage for not having good work ethic as you get older
- Selling drugs Now this is a big one, because it was a gateway to a whole lot of problems. A lot of people might say I'm only selling weed etc. but if your selling drugs you have to worry about getting robbed, and or getting shot while being robbed. Then you have to watch for the police and scammers and so much more negativity. It's a whole lot more work and risk than just working legit. I can honestly say I made a lot of money hustling

and had some good times, but the consequences caught up with me and they were far greater than the gains. A lot of people don't make it far in the street life, do your research. I thought that I was different but I wasn't, I'm here with guys with the same street life stories.

The time I've already done and still doing in prison, I can never get back. If I would have worked legally or went to school to further my education, I would have had far more to show for my life right now. As I think about it, the lifestyle I chose was stupid. It was crazy for me to risk my life for a quick monetary gain. I can always make more money, but I can never get those lost years back. You may be thinking, I'll do things smarter than he did, or I'm not going to get caught, but if you do, is the risk really worth it?

In closing, I say to the youth out there that you need to think about your future because everything you do now leads up to the man or woman you plan to be. Life is short, you don't want to waste years out of your life like I did. I wish you much success on your journey. I hope you think about the choices you make before you act on them. Don't let your bad attitude, being in your feelings or what others may think, sway you into making bad decisions. Because at the end of the day, you're going to be the one paying the consequences, while those people who were looking on/cheering you on are moving on with their lives. The Sky is the limit, don't let your environment stop you from reaching greatness. It's ok to stay legit. A legit guy got my girl right now.

STAY FREE

An Open Letter

TO THE YOUTH OF AMERICA,

First and foremost, I pray that all is well with you all and that this notation reaches you all in the best of health and a mind state conducive to your growth and development and well-being. My name is Richard Gray-EL and I'm a 37 year old Baltimore native who has been incarcerated for the past 16 years. My purpose in addressing you all today is to: 1. Inform you; 2. Encourage you; and 3. Incite you. Firstly, I want to enlighten you about the pitfalls of prison and why it is of the utmost importance to never fall victim to its grips. Many of us have had and have a disillusioned perception of what prison was and is, and was and is aware of real dangerous and harm that it can be to the human psyche. We have been told, as young boys that it is a rite of passage into manhood; and to the young sisters, that it's a part of life that we go through coming up how and where we do. I am here to say that what we have been told is a falsehood. Prison is not a game! It is not some fun place you would want to come to when you want to hang out with your buddies.

Furthermore, it is only a place that the uncivilized and unconscious find themselves at. It is a place that is designed to weaken your spirit and break you mentally; A place filled with injustice and unproductivity; A place full of unrest, misery, and despair; and a place full of isolation, insanity, and death. Growing up in the City of Baltimore, we have been subjected to all sorts of calamities, trials and tribulations, and atrocities. Be it coming up in a broken home, being raised in a drug and crime infested neighborhood, or even being raised by unproductive parents who have no idea of their importance to our growth and development. With those things we are all too familiar with. That contributes largely to our desperate states and lack of focus which allow us to fall victim to the perils of the streets which in turn can and will lead us to a life full of prison stints. Understanding this, we must not lose courage and our hope of living a successful life. Moreover, we must not stop believing in the greatness within ourselves as well the greatness that lies in others. Due to a lack of healthy alternatives, we have made many unwise and consequential decisions that have cost us more than we bargained for. Some have lost their homes, friends, family, minds, and some have even lost their lives. Yet even with all that turmoil surrounding us, all is not lost! I say that because every day we rise with the use of our limbs and mental faculties; we have an opportunity to be better. All we must do is seize that moment and let our dissatisfaction drive and motivate us to move in a different direction.

No longer can we allow the abnormal to pass as normal; No longer can we allow the seeds of prosperity within us to go uncultivated; No longer can we continue to victimize ourselves with oppression and injustice. No! We must combat against all those mentioned issues. We must combat all levels of disparity and illiteracy; we must remove all states of ignorance and comptonization; we must remove all barriers that thwart our expression of our True Selves, Young Brothers and Sisters, it starts with YOU! Do not continue to follow after false idols, false leaders, and especially false friends. It will only lead you on a continuous path of destruction. So remember, prison is just a mirror reflection of the chaotic societies we come up in. If you're dissatisfied with it out there then you'll definitely be dissatisfied by it in here.

So in closing, know that this is a fight that we must combat. For where there is Unity there is strength. Together we stand, divided we'll fall. Stay strong and Stay Free.

Peace, R. Gray-EL

From the Desk of: J Ghost Entertainment To: The Young Adults of America

From: Author Dr. Jachin B. Walls/Behind the Wall Mentor Subject: Against All Odds

I give a salute with a firm posture to the youth and young adults of America. I pray that this epistle will find you at a place in your life where you're at a crossroad to make a decision about your future. I am serving a Life plus Twenty-Three year sentence in a Maryland prison for which I'm not proud of. I am a Behind the Wall mentor with an autobiography coming out titled "Behind these Walls". The book is geared to help and encourage anybody who felt as though from a child that they didn't get a fair shake at life. My purpose in writing is to bring about healing to a hurting society. A society where it feels like the hope is gone for our children of tomorrow. I want to put a stop in the pain to prison pipeline for our youth.

My book titled "Behind These Walls", also has a Spanish version to follow, Detras de estos "Muros". It is a book about the struggles of a young child with troubling issues in the home which today's youth can identify with. The feeling of abandonment, depression and low self-esteem just to name a few can in turn cause a person to go into a dark place. Only to find oneself in the system created for us to fail, prison.

Prison offers so many things or might I say penitentiary. The base word is penitent. It has been a place of reform and atonement.

Remember this; I put a lot of effort in trying to build street cred. It didn't amount to much. What happened was that I left my sons and daughter to fend for themselves. I left their mothers to raise them on their own with other males to play my part. This is not what you want. (19) Years of seeing the same people,. same routine, same food, people who say they love you, family dying, and your life slipping away as you age Behind the Walls. The life that you're living won't last long. Prison's not for you. Get your education, I earned my doctorate degree in Christian Theology so that I can better myself, and help others see that there's a better way to live. Regardless of where you at, you have a bright future in front of you. Know who you are and whose you are. God created you with a greater purpose in mind than where you may currently find yourself. I believe in you. When was the last time someone invested in you? Well, I want to in- vest in you by speaking life to you. You are special, you're loved by somebody who sees the real you behind the mask. I'm here to help. Prison has limited boundaries, but the pen will continue to stroke paper with healing in mind for your soul and spirit.

Behind These Walls gives the reader a detailed account how I found what I was stripped of for years. Which was a strong sense of worth and love from God the Father, and his son Jesus the Christ. It's available to you, a relationship with him who will never leave you or forsake you.

Thank you and God Bless
Dr. Jachin B. Walls SR.

BEHIND THE WALL MENTORS CONTACT INFORMATION

Mr. Shawn Gardner shawngardner2012@gmail.com
Facebook/ real author Shawn Gardner
Twitter /authorshawngardner
Mr. Terry L. Carter II terrylcarter2@gmail.com
Dr. Jachin B. Walls SR. MinisterJachin@gmail.com
Mr. Marco Lomax mdlomax308@gmail.com
Mr. Andre Young andremy630@gmail.com
Mr. Richard Gray-El Richard.grayel@gmail.com

SPONSORED BY:

www.focusmovers.com   www.Rocmeg.com   www.iCARReFound.org

Morals & Principle Pals Curriculum Unit

Law Office of Gregory W Gardner
Phone# 303-552-2979

The Law Offices Of Natalie Finegar
Phone# 443-990-1809
NATALIE@FINEGARLAW.COM

Morals & Principle Pals Enterprise
themoralsandprinciplepals@gmail.com

NEWS

ARTICLES ON BALTIMORE CITY
POLICE OFFICERS FROM:

www.justice.gov/usao-md

&

www.baltimoresun.com

Marco Lomax

United States Department of Justice   Office of the United States Attorney

---

THE UNITED STATES ATTORNEY'S OFFICE

DISTRICT *of* MARYLAND

Search

SEARCH

HOME   ABOUT   NEWS   U.S. ATTORNEY   PRIORITIES   PROGRAMS   EMPLOYMENT

CONTACT US

U.S. Attorneys » District of Maryland » News

Department of Justice
U.S. Attorney 's Office District of Maryland

FOR IMMEDIATE RELEASE   Wednesday, March 1, 2017

Seven Baltimore City Police Officers Arrested for Abusing Power in Federal Racketeering Conspiracy

Officers Allegedly Robbed Victims, Filed False Affidavits and Made Fraudulent Overtime Claims; One Officer Also Charged in Separate Six-Defendant Drug Conspiracy Indictment

"Criminals Who Work in Police Agencies Unfairly Tarnish Honorable Officers"

Baltimore, Maryland - Federal agents arrested seven Baltimore City Police Department (BPD) officers today for a racketeering conspiracy and racketeering offenses, including robbery, extortion , and overtime fraud. The indictment was returned on February 23, 2017, and unsealed today following the execution of arrest and search warrants. One of the officers also was charged in a separate drug conspiracy indictment, also unsealed today.

The indictments were announced by Maryland U.S. Attorney Rod J. Rosenstein; Special Agent in Charge Gordon B. Johnson of the Federal Bureau of Investigation, Baltimore Field Office; Assistant Special Agent in Charge Don A. Hibbert of the Drug Enforcement Administration, Baltimore District Office; and Commissioner Kevin Davis of the Baltimore Police Department.

"This is not about aggressive policing, it is about a criminal conspiracy," said U.S. Attorney Rod J. Rosenstein. "Prosecuting criminals who work in police agencies is essential both to protect victims and to support the many honorable officers whose reputations they unfairly tarnish."

"As evidenced by these indictments the FBI will continue to make rooting out corruption at all levels one of its top criminal priorities," said Special Agent in Charge Gordon B. Johnson, FBI Baltimore Field Office. "Coupled with strong leadership by Commissioner Davis and his department, this investigation has dismantled a group of police officers who were besmirching the good name of the Baltimore City Police Department."

"The police officers charged today with crimes that erode trust with our community have disgraced the Baltimore Police Department and our profession," said Baltimore Police Commissioner Kevin Davis. "We will not shy away from accountability, as our community and the men and women who serve our City every day with pride and integrity deserve nothing less. Our investigative partnership with the FBI will continue as we strive to improv. Reform isn't always a pretty thing to watch unfold, but it's necessary in our journey toward a police department our City deserves."

DEFENDANTS

The officers charged in the racketeering indictment are:

> Detective Momodu Bondeva Kenton Gondo, a/k/a GMoney and Mike, age 34, of Owings Mills, Maryland;
> Detective Evodio Calles Hendrix, age 32, of Randallstown, Maryland;
> Detective Daniel Thomas Hers!, age 47, of Joppa, Maryland; Sergeant Wayne Earl Jenkins, age 36, of Middle River, Maryland;
> Detective Jemell Lamar Rayam, age 36, of Owings Mills;
> Detective Marcus Roosevelt Taylor, age 30, of Glen Burnie; and
> Detective Maurice Kilpatrick Ward, age 36, of Middle River.

A separate indictment alleges that Detective Gondo joined a drug-dealing conspiracy. In addition to Gondo, the other indictment charges:

> Antonio Shropshire, a/k/a Brill, B, and Tony, age 31, of Baltimore;
> Omari Thomas, a/k/a Lil' Bril, Lil B, and Chewy, age 25, of Middle River;
> Antoine Washington, a/k/a Twan, age 27, of Baltimore;
> Alexander Campbell, a/k/a Munch, age 28, of Baltimore; and Glen Kyle Wells, a/k/a Lou, and Kyle, age 31, of Baltimore.

RACKETEERING INDICTMENT

The racketeering indictment alleges that the police officers stole money, property and narcotics from victims, some of whom had not committed crimes; swore out false affidavits; submitted false official incident reports; and engaged in large-scale time and attendance fraud.

Count One, racketeering conspiracy, alleges robbery and extortion violations committed by the defendants in 2015 and 2016 when they were officers in the police department's Gun Trace Task Force, a specialized unit created to investigate firearms crimes.

Count Two, a substantive racketeering charge, alleges those crimes as well as several incidents of robbery and extortion committed by five of the seven defendants beginning in 2015, before they joined the task force. Four of the defendants previously worked together in another police unit; a fifth defendant was working in a separate unit during the earlier incidents.

In some cases, there was no evidence of criminal conduct by the victims; the officers stole money that had been earned lawfully. In other instances, narcotics and firearms were recovered from arrestees. In several instances, the defendants did not file any police reports. The amounts stolen ranged from $200 to $200,000.

According to the indictment, the defendants schemed to steal money, property, and narcotics by detaining victims, entering residences, conducting traffic stops, and swearing out false search warrant affidavits. In addition, the defendants allegedly prepared and submitted false official incident and arrest reports, reports of property seized from arrestees, and charging documents. The false reports concealed the fact that the officers had stolen money, property and narcotics from individuals.

The indictment alleges that the defendants obstructed law enforcement by alerting each other about potential investigations of their criminal conduct, coaching one another to give false testimony to investigators from the Internal Investigations Division of the BPD, and turning off their body cameras to avoid recording encounters with civilians. Finally, the indictment alleges that the defendants defrauded the BPD and the State of Maryland by submitting false time and attendance records in order to obtain salary and overtime payments for times when the defendants did not work.

For example, according to the indictment, on July 8, 2016, Rayam submitted an affidavit for a search warrant which falsely stated that he, Jenkins and Gonda had conducted a full day of surveillance at the residence of two victims. Later that day, Rayam, Gonda and Hersl conducted a traffic stop of the victims during which Rayam allegedly stole $3.400 in cash. Rayam, Gonda and Hersl then transported the victims to a BPD off-site facility. In a telephone call, Jenkins told Gonda that he would meet them at the facility and that they should introduce Jenkins as the U.S. Attorney. When Jenkins arrived, he told one of the victims that he was a federal officer. Jenkins and Rayam asked the victim if he had any money in his residence, and the victim said he had $70,000 in cash. Jenkins, Rayam, Gonda and Hersl then transported the victims back to their home. In the master bedroom closet, the officers located two heat sealed bundles - one containing $50, 000 and the other containing $20,000 in $100 bills. Jenkins, Rayam, Gonda and Hersl stole the $20,000 bundle. Gonda and Rayam later argued about how to divide the stolen money. On July 11, 2016 , Gonda deposited $8,000 in cash into his checking account.

Three days after the robbery, on July 11, 2016, Jenkins went on vacation with his family in Myrtle Beach, South Carolina, staying until July 16, 2016. The indictment alleges that Jenkins falsely claimed he worked overtime on five of the six days he was on vacation. That same week, Gonda called Rayam and said that working for the BPD was "easy money" and that "one hour can be eight hours." referring to working for one hour and then claiming eight hours on official time and attendance records.

In another episode alleged in the Indictment, on September 7, 2016, Rayam described to Gonda how he had told Jenkins that he only "taxed" a detainee a "little bit." referring to stealing some but not all of the detainee's drug proceeds. Rayam said that they had not arrested the victim, so he "won't say nothing." Rayam told Gonda that he had to give Wayne Jenkins $100 of the money stolen from the victim. The victim was not charged.

DRUG INDICTMENT

In a separate seven-count indictment, Gonda, Shropshire, Thomas, Washington, Campbell and Wells are charged with conspiracy to distribute and possess with intent to distribute heroin as part of the Shropshire drug trafficking organization (OTO). Washington is charged with possession with intent to distribute and distribution of heroin resulting in death; Shropshire, Gonda, and Campbell are charged with possession with intent to distribute heroin; and Shropshire is also charged with possession with intent to distribute heroin and cocaine. According to the indictment, the conspirators primarily distributed heroin near the Alameda Shopping Center in Baltimore.

In one telephone call, Detective Gonda allegedly said, "I sell drugs." In addition to selling heroin, Gonda provided sensitive law enforcement information to other conspirators in order to help the OTO and protect his co-conspirators. For example, Gonda helped Shropshire get rid of a GPS tracking device that had been placed on his vehicle by DEA Gonda also advised Wells about law enforcement operations in order to protect Wells from being arrested.

CONCLUSION

Anyone who believes they may have information about these cases is urged to call 1-800-CALL FBI (1-800-225-5324).

The seven defendants charged in the racketeering conspiracy each face a maximum sentence of 20 years in prison for the conspiracy and for racketeering. The defendants are expected to have an initial appearance in U.S. District Court in Baltimore later today.

Shropshire, Washington, and Campbell each face a mandatory minimum of 10 years and up to life in prison for conspiracy to distribute at least one kilogram of heroin. Gonda, Wells, and Thomas each face a mandatory five years and up to 40 years in prison for conspiracy to distribute at least 100 grams of heroin. Washington faces a maximum penalty of 20 years in prison for distribution of heroin resulting in death. Shropshire, Gonda, and Campbell also face a maximum penalty of 20 years in prison for possession with intent to distribute heroin and cocaine.

An indictment is not a finding of guilt. An individual charged by indictment is presumed innocent unless and until proven guilty at some later criminal proceedings.

United States Attorney Rod J. Rosenstein commended the FBI and Baltimore Police Department for their work in both investigations, and the DEA for its work in the drug investigation. U.S. Attorney Rosenstein also recognized the Baltimore County Police Department and Harford County Sheriff's Office for their assistance in the racketeering case. Mr. Rosenstein thanked Assistant U.S. Attorneys Leo J. Wise and Derek E. Hines, who are prosecuting these Organized Crime Drug Enforcement Task Force cases.

Topic(s):
Drug Trafficking Public Corruption

Component(s):
USAO - Maryland

United States Department of Justice   Office of the United States Attorney

---

THE UNITED STATES ATTORNEY'S OFFICE

DISTRICT *of* MARYLAND

U.S. Attorneys » District of Maryland » News

Department of Justice
U.S. Attorney 's Office District of Maryland

FOR IMMEDIATE RELEASE   Thursday, July 6, 2017

Indicted Baltimore City Police Officers Charged With Additional Robberies

Two Civilian Defendants Charged With Committing Robbery With Indicted Baltimore City Police Officer

July 6, 2017
 FOR IMMEDIATE RELEASE   **Contact ELIZABETH MORSE**
 www.justice.gov/usao/md   **at (410) 209-4885**

Baltimore, Maryland - A federal grand jury returned a superseding indictment charging three previously indicted Baltimore City Police Officers with additional robberies. The superseding indictment charges the defendants with racketeering conspiracy, racketeering, robbery, extortion, and possession of a firearm in furtherance of a crime of violence . The superseding indictment was unsealed today and charges the following defendants :

Sergeant Wayne Earl Jenkins, age 37, of Middle River, Maryland; Detective Daniel Thomas Hers!, age 48, of Joppa, Maryland; and Detective Marcus Roosevelt Taylor, age 30, of Glen Burnie, Maryland.

A federal grand jury also returned a separate indictment charging two additional defendants, who are not police officers but were posing as police officers , with robbing two Baltimore City residents and with brandishing a firearm during a crime of violence. The indictment alleges that the two named defendants committed the robbery with a Baltimore City police officer. The second indictment was unsealed today and charges the

103

following defendants:

Thomas Robert Finnegan, age 38, of Easton, Pennsylvania; and David Kendall Rahim, age 41, of Baltimore, Maryland.

Defendants Jenkins, Hersl, and Taylor had previously been ordered detained pending trial. Defendants Finnegan and Rahim will have their initial appearances in court today.

The superseding indictment and indictment were announced by Acting United States Attorney for the District of Maryland Stephen M. Schenning and Special Agent in Charge Gordon B. Johnson of the Federal Bureau of Investigation, Baltimore Field Office.

SUPERSEDING INDICTMENT

The 6-count superseding indictment alleges that Jenkins, Hersl, and Taylor engaged in 13 robberies, extortion and time and attendance fraud. According to the superseding indictment, beginning in 2011, the defendants stole money, property, and narcotics by detaining victims, entering residences, conducting traffic stops, and swearing out false search warrant affidavits.

For example, as charged in the superseding indictment, in spring 2015, Jenkins stole at least 20 pounds of high-quality marijuana and at least $20,000 from two individuals who were conducting a drug sale at Belvedere Towers in Baltimore City. Jenkins falsely told the buyer and seller that he was a Drug Enforcement Agency (DEA) agent, to conceal his identity, and that he was seizing the money and drugs and would make a decision about whether to charge them later. Jenkins then drove Taylor and a co-defendant to a wooded area off Northern Parkway and gave them $5,000 each from the stolen money. After the incident, Jenkins went to a strip club in Baltimore County where he robbed a stripper.

Similarly, as charged in the superseding indictment, in summer 2016 Hersl stole money from the car of an arrestee. Hersl drove one of his co-defendants to the parking lot of a local high school, which was near the incident, and gave him a portion of the stolen money. While Hersl and the co-defendant were splitting the stolen money, Jenkins broke into the arrestee's storage unit and stole 2 kilograms of cocaine.

The superseding indictment alleges that in June 2016 Jenkins believed that a co-defendant owed him money, so Jenkins gave the co-defendant drugs and a firearm that had been seized in a law enforcement operation , and told him to sell them. The co-defendant, along with another co- defendant, sold the firearm to a drug dealer.

The superseding indictment also alleges that the defendants committed systemic time and attendance fraud, including claiming overtime when they were at home and on vacation .

According to the superseding indictment, between spring 2011 and October 2016 , the defendants allegedly conducted 13 separate robberies, taking over $280,000 in US currency, more than 2 kilograms of cocaine, other narcotics, a 9mm handgun, a $4,000 wristwatch, and other property.

The superseding indictment alleges that the defendants obstructed law enforcement by alerting each other about potential investigations of their criminal conduct , and turning off their body cameras to avoid recording encounters with civilians.

ROBBERY INDICTMENT

Thomas Robert Finnegan and David Kendall Rahim were indicted on charges of conspiracy, robbery, and possession of a firearm during a crime of violence.

On June 27, 2014, police officers with the BPD's Gun Trace Task Force, executed a search warrant on a store in the Brooklyn neighborhood of Baltimore City. During the search, one of the police officers asked whether there was any large amounts of money in the store. The storeowner indicated that she had $20,000 in cash in her pocketbook that she was intending to use to pay off a tax liability. At this point, members of GTTF did not make arrests, nor seize anything from the property. Later that day, a member of the GTTF informed Finnegan and Rahim about the money and they agreed to set up a robbery at the home of the store owner. Using a law enforcement database, the GTTF detective located the home address of the victims. The defendants surveilled the house, agreed to impersonate the police when conducting the home invasion, and were given tactical gear by the Detective. The GTTF detective remained outside in the vehicle so that he could intercept any police officers who responded to the home invasion by telling them he was a BPD officer. Finnegan and Rahim entered the residence and robbed the victims at gunpoint of the $20,000.

REARRAIGNMENTS

The following four Baltimore City Police, who were previously indicted, have rearraignments scheduled for the following dates:

Detective Momodu Bondeva Kenton Gondo, age 34, of Owings Mills, Maryland - October 12, 2017; Detective Evodio Calles Hendrix, age 32, of Randallstown, Maryland - July 21, 2017;

Detective Jemell Lamar Rayam, age 36, of Owings Mills, Maryland - November 9, 2017; and Detective Maurice Kilpatrick Ward, age 36, of Middle River, Maryland - July 24, 2017.

Defendant Gondo's rearraignment has been scheduled in the RICO case and a separate drug trafficking conspiracy with non-BPD defendants.

An indictment is not a finding of guilt. An individual charged by indictment is presumed innocent unless and until proven guilty at some later criminal proceedings.

Acting United States Attorney Stephen M. Schenning commended the FBI for its work in the investigation. Mr. Schenning thanked Assistant U.S. Attorneys Leo J. Wise and Derek E. Hines, who are prosecuting these Organized Crime Drug Enforcement Task Force cases.

Component(s):   **USAO - Maryland**

Lawsuit, indictment detail alleged false imprisonment, theft of couple by Baltimore gun task force officers

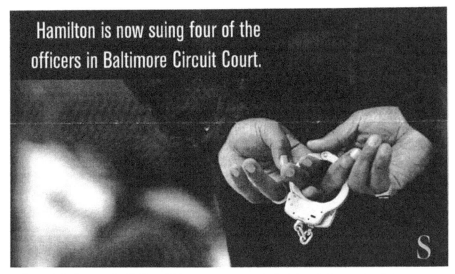

Hamilton is now suing four of the officers in Baltimore Circuit Court.

Lawsuit, indictment detail alleged false imprisonment, theft of Carroll County couple by Baltimore gun task force officers. (Baltimore Sun Video)

By Justin Fenton
The Baltimore Sun

SEPTEMBER 20, 20i7, 10:45 f\M

A Carroll County woman is suing members of a rogue Baltimore Police Department unit, the first civil claim since the officers were indicted over a series of robberies and extortions.

The complaint filed in Baltimore Circuit Court by Nancy Hamilton seeks at least $9oo,ooo in damages, and the city has appointed lawyers to defend the officers. With other attorneys exploring similar legal claims, taxpayers are on the hook for legal fees and potential damages awarded in the civil courts.

While running errands with her husband in Baltimore County, Hamilton was pulled over by men in police vests who put them in handcuffs, placed them in separate vehicles and took her husband into a darkened old school building for an hour, according to the lawsuit and federal prosecutors. Hamilton said she thought she had been abducted by

107

police impersonators.

The four officers named in the complaint are among eight members of the Baltimore Police Department's elite Gun Trace Task Force who have been charged with racketeering and other federal crimes. Two of the eight have pleaded guilty. Two others are expected to plead guilty in coming weeks, including two of the officers named in Hamilton's complaint. The rest have pleaded not guilty.

Hamiton's allegations involve an incident documented in detail in the March indictment and partially captured by wiretaps. Taken together, they provide new insight into how far some officers allegedly went in pursuit of their targets.

Wiretaps captured the supervisor of the unit instructing another officer to tell the Hamilton's he was a federal prosecutor, according to the federal indictment , while both the complaint and indictment say Ronald Hamilton was interrogated inside the former Pimlico Middle School building , which is used as the police training academy facility. The Police Department refused to discuss whether the facility is regularly used for interrogations.

"They never cut on any of the lights," Hamilton's attorney, James Rhodes, said in an interview. Attorneys hired by the city to represent the officers in the civil case declined to comment.

The four officers named in the complaint are Detective Jemell Rayam, Detective Momodu Gondo, Sgt. Wayne Jenkins and Detective Daniel Hersl.

On July 8, 2016, Rayam applied for and received a search warrant of the Hamilton's Carroll County home using information federal authorities now say was falsified. The affidavit claimed that Rayam, Gonda and Jenkins had conducted a full day of surveillance on Ronald Hamilton, but prosecutors say Gondo and Rayam were at their homes when they claimed to be watching him.

"He [Jenkins] gave the order; we're pulling them over," Rayam was recorded saying around 3 p.m., according to the indictment. "We pull them over, bring them back to the academy. That's per Sergeant Jenko," he said, allegedly referring to Jenkins.

Rayam, Gonda and Hersl conducted a traffic stop of the Hamilton's on or near Reisterstown Road in Baltimore County, and they were removed from their vehicle "without consent and in fear of being beaten or worse," Nancy Hamilton's complaint alleges.

Jenkins and Hersl have pleaded not guilty; Rayam and Gondo also have pleaded not guilty but have rearraignment hearings scheduled later this year to change their pleas.

Prosecutors say Rayam asked Ronald Hamilton, who has twice served federal prison sentences for drug convictions, "Where's the money?" Federal prosecutors say he had $3,400 in cash on him, which Raya m allegedly stole.

Nancy Hamilton's complaint says the couple were handcuffed and placed in separate vehicles.

"We are headed down now [to a BPD off-site facility]," Gonda said in a phone call to Jenkins, according to the indictment. "We go, um, got the package," he said, using coded language for having taken Hamilton into custody. "I got the, um, male, and they got the female."

"Okay, hey, uh, did you tell them anything at all?" Jenkins asked. "No," Gonda said.

"All right. Just tell them you gotta wait for the U.S. Attorney. When I get there, treat me like I'm the [expletive] U.S. Attorney. Like, hey sir, how are you, we got our target in pocket," Jenkins said. "And then introduce me as the U.S. Attorney."

The off-site facility was the training academy. Specialized units within the agency use trailers on the property as offices, but a spokesman for the Police Department could not point to any policies or procedures that allow such units to interrogate suspects at the training academy.

According to the indictment, Ronald Hamilton was interviewed by Rayam and Jenkins, who pretended to be a federal agent. Outside, Nancy Hamilton complained that she needed to use the bathroom and she was taken inside. The building was "very dark and appeared to be closed," her complaint says. She "continued to be nervous and fearful for her life as she was taken in the training facility."

During the interrogation, the officers asked if Hamilton had any money in his home, and Hamilton said he had $70,000 in cash.

"Jenkins told him, you take care of us, we take care of you, or words to that effect," and asked Hamilton to identify someone the officers could rob, federal prosecutors wrote in the indictment.

Ronald Hamilton has a long record of drug offenses, and in the late 1990s was described by federal agents in court documents as "the person who controlled most of the drug trafficking in West and Southwest Baltimore City and county." But Ronald Hamilton would later say he has stayed out of trouble since his release three years ago, and was making money buying vehicles at auctions and selling them for a profit, as well as renting out properties.

After the officers drove the Hamilton's to their home, Ronald Hamilton directed the officers to a master bedroom closet, where he had $70,000 in two heat-sealed bundles, according to the federal indictment. One package allegedly contained $50,000; another had $20,000. The officers allegedly took the $20,000 bundle, then contacted a Carroll County drug task force to join in the operation. The $50,000 package was seized by the Carroll officers as alleged drug proceeds.

Prosecutors allege that Rayam called Gondo at 10:45 p.m. that night to discuss the money they had stolen. Rayam allegedly wrote a false incident report, without disclosing the money that had been taken at the traffic stop or from the home. Three days later, Gondo deposited $8,ooo in cash into his personal bank account, the indictment says.

Ronald Hamilton fought to get the money seized by Carroll authorities back. In court, county prosecutors alleged that Hamilton had obtained the money from a heroin deal. Hamilton said that the money was legitimate and that his prior criminal record had caused him to be "unfairly and unjustly" targeted.

He was able to produce what Carroll prosecutors believed was sufficient documentation for $30,000 of the cash, which was returned to him, but officials kept the other $20,000.

Hamilton's attorney in the forfeiture case, Gary Desper, said that changed when the indictment against the officers came down. Carroll prosecutors then returned the $20,000 as well, saying, "We don't want anything to do with that," Desper said.

jfenton@baltsun.com
twitter.com/Justin-fenton

Prosecutors drop dozens more cases involving indicted officers

BY KEVIN RECTOR THE BALTIMORE SUN

Prosecutors in Baltimore have decided to drop dozens of additional criminal cases that relied on the testimony of eight city police officers indicted on federal racketeering charges, bringing the total to more than 100, Baltimore State's Attorney Marilyn J. Mosby's office said Tuesday.

And they have dropped still more cases that relied on the testimony of officers in police body camera footage that critics say showed improper or questionable behavior.

Overall, more than 850 criminal cases in Baltimore "have been or potentially will be impacted" as a result of the federal racketeering case and three separate body-camera investigations, Mosby's office said. Hundreds of cases are still being reviewed.

The figures were announced in a written statement released by Mosby's office Tuesday evening. She was quoted as saying, "As prosecutors, we will remain vigilant in our pursuit of justice and we will continue to do our part to restore public trust and build confidence in the criminal justice system."

The updated figures reflect the growing fallout from scandals that have cast the Baltimore Police Department in a negative light in recent months, just as it seeks to implement sweeping reforms under a court-enforced consent decree with the U.S. Department of Justice.

Mosby's office said the figures are the result of local prosecutors' efforts to "thoroughly evaluate" not only cases in which questionable police activity arises, but also every other criminal case that is dependent on the word of officers who have been involved in questionable activity.

Deborah Katz Levi, director of special litigation in the Baltimore public defender's office, which helped uncover some of the body-camera footage, said that while she applauds the "initial efforts" by Mosby's office to address alleged police misconduct, prosecutors haven't gone far enough.

"[We] believe their numbers are far too low and there are still far too. many individuals incarcerated on tainted convictions," Levi said. "The state's attorney's office refuses to disclose names of officers involved in the third video, and we think they are constitutionally obligated to do so. In addition, they have yet to disclose how they have arrived at these totals and our office has calculated much greater numbers of affected convictions. We continue to encourage transparency and dialogue as we work to undo as many tainted convictions as possible."

T.J. Smith, a police spokesman, said police "are continuing to work to address the concerns that have been brought forth as a result of these situations." Smith stressed the federal indictment and the three body camera cases an=- each "unique and independent of each other."

He said the cases involving body camera footage are "still being investigated and no criminal wrongdoing has been proven. "Federal prosecutors charged seven officers in March and an eighth last month on federal racketeering charges, alleging they colluded to rob citizens, filed false court paperwork and put in for fraudulent overtime.

Over the course of the past several months, body-camera footage has come out from three separate incidents that prosecutors say raise significant questions about police conduct.

Defense counsel have suggested officers can be seen planting evidence in the videos, while the Police Department has suggested the officers were merely "re-creating" legitimate discoveries of narcotics that they had forgotten to record.

Prosecutors have said the footage raises significant credibility issues for the officers involved, leading to the decisions to drop cases. At least one officer involved in one of the drug busts has argued in an internal memo to his superiors that the bust was entirely legitimate.

Similar credibility issues were raised for the indicted officers. Two of those officers have pleaded guilty; others maintain their innocence.

Because of the federal charges against officers, a total of 109 criminal cases have been dropped or will be dropped, Mosby's office said.

Another 88 cases remain under review. Prosecutors have decided to move forward with four cases with links to the indicted officers, on the strength of other evidence.

As a result of the body camera footage, at least 213 cases have been dropped or will be dropped, and dozens more could be, Mosby's office said.

At least another 170 cases -both closed and open -remain under review, prosecutors said.

Prosecutors have determined to move forward with at least 67 cases linked to the officers in the body-earner .a cases, on the strength of other evidence.

Mosby's office has not described the cases involved or the nature of the crimes alleged in them.

David Rocah, senior attorney with the American Civil Liberties Union, said Tuesday evening that the numbers as released by Mosby's office do not seem to add up, and were confusing.

He said the officers involved "have destroyed their credibility," which Mosby's office "seems to recognize."

He also said he is "flabbergasted" by Police Commissioner Kevin Davis' past suggestion that what the body-camera footage reveals is not the planting of evidence, but the recreation of legitimate drug discoveries.

Either way, it is "a huge problem" and is "still lying," Rocah said, and "if any other actor in our justice system did it, even with the best of motivations, they would be prosecuted, disbarred, etc. Why are police held to a different standard?"

Rocah said he doesn't understand why officers haven't at least been charged administratively with violating police policies.

"The Police Department's entire response to this has been so beyond inadequate, and has made clear that all the words spoken about the need to hold officers accountable mean absolutely nothing," he said.

krector@baltsun.com
twitter.com/rectorsun

ABOUT THE AUTHOR

Marco Lomax is a man of many mistakes, but strives to be a better man each and everyday he wakes up. He's a Behind the Wall Mentor, and is devoted to helping out younger individuals headed down the road he has traveled. Mr. Lomax has always appeared as a leader and considered a responsible, loyal, trust worthy young man. He puts forth a hard working effort in what ever he intends to do, and is very family oriented. He enjoys playing basketball, traveling, and reading. He also enjoys helping out those in need and/or are less fortunate. Mr. Lomax is a God-fearing man who knows that as long as he has faith in God and continues to change for the better to set the example for those who look up to him, he will leave a legacy of a life well-lived.

Made in the USA
Middletown, DE
03 July 2023

34547398R00070